MEDIEVAL
INSTRUMENTAL
DANCES

Music: Scholarship and Performance
Thomas Binkley, General Editor

Dance in the Garden of Mirth, Guillaume de Lorris and Jean de Meun, *Le Roman de la Rose* (ca. 1380). Oxford). Oxford, Bodleian Library, MS E. Mus. 65, fol. 3v.

MEDIEVAL INSTRUMENTAL DANCES

TIMOTHY J. McGEE

INDIANA UNIVERSITY PRESS
Bloomington and Indianapolis

Manufactured in the United States of America

Library of Congress Cataloging-in-Publication Data

Medieval instrumental dances.

Music—scholarship and performance.
Texts of the 2 vocal works in Old French.
"Includes all of the compositions that are known or
suspected to be instrumental dances from before
ca. 1430"—p.
Includes list of sources and bibliographical
references.
1. Dance music—500–1400.   2. Dance music—15th
century.   I. McGee, Timothy J. (Timothy James)
II. Series.

M2.M2788   1989   88-45498
ISBN 0-253-33353-9

2   3   4   5   6   01   00   99   98   97

CONTENTS

THE DANCES

PLATES

Preface

This study of medieval dance music has occupied me on and off for over fifteen years and has led me down interesting paths of investigation that I had not originally imagined would be relevant. It has broadened my knowledge in a number of directions, and I sincerely hope that the information presented here will contribute not only to the reader's knowledge of medieval dance music but also to an appreciation of the complexity and scope of medieval secular culture and the place of dance in daily life during those centuries.

This edition contains all the compositions known or suspected to be instrumental dances from before ca. 1430. In addition to pieces with dance names, I have included all instrumental compositions found in the company of dances. Two texted pieces are also edited here: "Kalenda Maya," because it is commonly thought to have existed first as an instrumental dance without text; and "Souvent souspire," because it is closely related to "Kalenda Maya."

My search did not always yield clear or unambiguous answers to the various problems. The extent of the influence from eastern Mediterranean cultures, for example, is fascinating and suggests a number of musical consequences, but it is clear to only some degree and in only certain aspects, leaving more questions than answers. In those cases where the existing evidence is incomplete and does not allow definitive answers I have not shied away from offering possible conclusions, but I have tried to make it clear that they are personal speculations. I view this book, therefore, not as the definitive writing on medieval instrumental dance music, but as a somewhat speculative study along the way to a complete understanding.

Acknowledgments

In the process of this study I have consulted a number of people who willingly gave advice and assistance. I am grateful to all of them, and acknowledge my debts: to Marcia Epstein, Robert Taylor, and Dennis McAuliffe, who assisted me with translations; to Margaret Bent, Thomas Binkley, Edmund Bowles, Ingrid Brainard, Fredrick Crane, Andrew Hughes, Timothy Rice, and George Sawa, who provided musicological assistance of various kinds; to the Toronto Consort and numerous other performers who played the dances and discussed the music. I am indebted to the Social Sciences and Humanities Research Council of Canada for supporting the research and for providing funds to have the music prepared. The final copy of the music was done by Robert Mazur using the MusScribe program developed by Keith Hamel.

MEDIEVAL INSTRUMENTAL DANCES

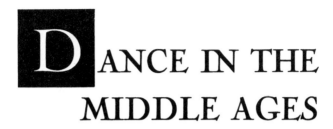

DANCE IN THE MIDDLE AGES

THE EVIDENCE

Curt Sachs describes and documents the tradition of dancing as a function of religious worship as well as recreation in many cultures from earliest recorded history.[1] During the early Middle Ages religious dancing often combined pagan and Christian ritual at weddings and funerals, at Shrovetide and on the first day of May.[2] Dancing continued to be a part of the Christian ceremony of worship throughout the era; church documents from the late Middle Ages make it clear that dances were permitted in the celebration of certain feasts and that they were performed by clerics.[3] Frequent prohibition by church administrators and councils suggests that dancing was not always approved, although the practice was recorded in some locations in Europe as late as the end of the seventeenth century, and it continues to this day in the tradition of some Basque communities.[4]

Information concerning secular dance in the late Middle Ages has survived in a variety of sources. Iconographic evidence, such as the manuscript miniatures and frescos reproduced in Plates 1–4 and the frontispiece, provides images of dancing individuals, couples, and groups. A few scattered letters and diaries survive from the period containing such entries as: "Each evening the Signore calls them together with the trumpets and harps and lutes, and he dances until two o'clock."[5] And a wealth of descriptions of dance can be found in the literature of the period, as in "Le Roman de la Violette": "The king who was so handsome and noble, arranged them well. After eating he sent them all carolling."[6] The following excerpts from three of the best-known fourteenth-century writers in England, France, and Italy further demonstrate the scope and variety to be found in literary references:

> Ful curteysly she called me,
> "What do ye there, beau sire?" quod she,
> "Come, and if it lyke you
> To dauncen, daunseth with vs now."

> And I, without taryeng,
> Went into the karollyng.
>
> —Chaucer[7]

Some sang pastourelles about Robichon and Amelot, others played on vielles chansons royal and estampies, dances and notas. On lute and psaltery each according to his preference [played] lais of love, descorts and ballads in order to entertain those who were ill.

—Maillart[8]

When they had put away the tables, since all the young men and women knew how to carol, play instruments and sing, and some of them really well, the queen commanded that the instruments be brought, and at her command Dioneo picked up a lute and Fiametta a vielle, and began sweetly to play a dance. At that, after they had sent their servants away to eat, the queen and the other women, together with two young men, made a circle and with slow steps began to dance the carol.

—Boccaccio[9]

All these kinds of evidence are helpful in providing a general impression of dance, but their use is limited. Archival sources such as those that attest to the presence of religious dancing are useful in determining the varieties of settings that included dance and some of the people who participated.[10] The iconography gives some details about dance formations, body position, costumes, and musical instruments: the frontispiece and Plates 1, 2, and 4 depict dancers holding hands in small groups, making graceful movements with their feet close to the floor; Plate 3 shows couples in graceful motion; and Plate 4 includes a young lady springing on her hands. The line of text beneath the illustration in the frontispiece speaks of dancing the carol. But the dances in the other pictures are not identified, and it would be dangerous to assume on such slight evidence that the small groups holding hands in the other pictures are also dancing carols. Such a conclusion may be possible after a thorough search of the iconography of dance, but unfortunately no complete study has been made of the subject.[11] At present we cannot be sure that the couples in Plate 3 are dancing at all; they may be merely processing in the garden. And the upside-down youth in Plate 4 may be a tumbler.

References in the letters and literature of the period supply names of dances and descriptions of dance formations, steps, instrumental accompaniment, and the occasions on which dancing took place. We can see in the earlier quotations, for example, that the carol was danced in all three countries, and that on occasion it followed dinner; Boccaccio even tells us that the dancers form a circle to dance the carol. Numerous additional quotations could be cited that would add minor refinements to the above information.[12] Thus, although little in the way of specific detail is available in these sources individually, as a group they fill in large portions of the picture; a mention of the dance formations here, a glimpse of a step there. As with iconography, a systematic study of these references would probably yield a surprising amount of information, but none has been undertaken.[13]

What one can learn from iconographic depictions of the vivid, frozen images

Plate 1. *The Effects of Good Government* (detail), Ambrogio Lorenzetti (1337–39). Siena, Palazzo Publico. Courtesy Art Resource.

Plate 2. *Church Militant* (detail), Andrea di Bonaiuto (1365). Florence, Spanish Chapel, Santa Maria Novella.

Plate 3. Fresco (ca. 1420). Trent, Castello del Buonconsiglio. Per
concessione del Museo Provinciale d'Arte di Trento.

Plate 4. *Music in the Garden of Delight,* Guillaume de Lorris and Jean de
Meun, *Le Roman de la Rose.* Valencia, Biblioteca Universitaria, MS 387, fol.
6v.

of dancers, and from the colorful literary descriptions, remains mostly at the general level. They do not provide the specifics of tempo, duration, and step sequence needed for a detailed understanding of medieval dance. But when combined with the theoretical sources and an analysis of the surviving dance repertory, even some of these facts can be deduced, and the composite picture assembled here, although still incomplete, contains far more details than had previously been suspected.

On a larger level, the surviving evidence also contributes to a perception of the general spirit of dance and its importance in the lives of the citizens of the late Middle Ages. The bulk of the information is in reference to the aristocracy, for it was they who commissioned the books and paintings and kept the records. (For these reasons it is probable that the music printed here is representative mostly of that class.) But occasionally there is a reference to other classes, from which we learn that dance was for all an important and frequent activity.

THEORETICAL STATEMENTS AND THE DANCE REPERTORY

Vocal and instrumental dances existed side by side throughout the era and obviously influenced one another; indeed it is not always possible to separate information about one from that for the other. The names and descriptions of some of the vocal and instrumental dances are identical, and it would appear that in terms of function and form they were closely related. In the discussion to follow, therefore, I have frequently pooled all available information about both vocal and instrumental dances in order to arrive at a better understanding of dancing in the Middle Ages and the nature of the music in this volume.

Vocal Dances

In the opinion of a number of scholars, the most popular secular poetic forms of the late Middle Ages were intimately connected with dance. Similarities have been noted between the poetic formal schemes and those of known dances.[14] Their names are also words used in connection with dancing, and it has been suggested that the names may have been derived from dances, although the etymological derivations are not certain nor is there agreement as to which came first, dance or poetic form: rondeau, rotta, rondellus, rond, round—round dance; balade, ballata—from the verb *balader*, *ballare*, to dance; *virelai*—from the verb *virer*, to twist; carola, karol, carole, querole—a circle or line dance.[15]

Secular music survives in all these forms. The bulk of the earliest surviving works are in the troubadour/trouvère repertory, and they remained popular secular forms in France, Italy, and England until the end of the fifteenth century. But these forms, which may have been dances in the twelfth and thirteenth centuries or earlier, seem to be quite removed from any association with dance music by the time we find most of the musical examples, in the fourteenth and fifteenth centuries. The later repertory is sophisticated art

music matching the theoretical descriptions of the formal design of the earlier
dance compositions, although rarely exhibiting the kind of melodic and
rhythmic patterns that would suggest the dances described in the earlier literary and theoretical accounts. The relationship of the earlier forms to the
more sophisticated later examples is demonstrated by some of the earliest
vocal dances with music, for example, the Latin rondeaux at the end of the
Florence copy of the Notre Dame repertory[16] (see Example 1). The illumination at the beginning of the fascicle depicts clerics in a "round" formation,
probably dancing; and Yvonne Rokseth suggests that the 56 compositions are
a repertory danced by clerics as a part of worship.[17]

The clearest theoretical description of vocal dances was written by Johannes
de Grocheio, in his *De Musica*, ca. 1300.[18] Although he does not name the
"rondeaux" specifically, his description of the round dance (*rotundellus*) clearly
fits that form. He requires the round to have a refrain whose melody is also

Example 1. "De Patre Principio," from Florence, Biblioteca Mediceo-
Laurenziana, Pluteo 29, 1, fol. 463r.

I

De Patre principio	From the Father in the beginning
Gaudeamus eya	Let us rejoice, eya
Filius principium	The Son was the beginning
Cum gloria	With glory
Novum pascha predicat ecclesia	The Church proclaims a new Pass-over.

II

Patris ex palacio	From the Father's palace
Gaudeamus . . .	
Matris in palacium	Into the mother's chamber
Cum gloria	
Novum . . .	

III

Pro mortis exilio	For the exile of death
Gaudeamus . . .	
Venit in exilium	He comes into exile
Cum gloria	
Novum . . .	

[four more verses]

Translation from Gordon A. Anderson, ed., *One Part Latin Conductus—The
Latin Repertoire*, Notre-Dame and Related Conductus, Opera Omnia, vol. 8
(Henryville, Ottawa, and Binningen: Institute of Mediaeval Music, n.d.), p.ii.

used in the verse.[19] As will be discussed below, this requirement separates the round dance from all other dance forms whose refrains are melodically different from their verses.[20] Example 1 conforms to Grocheio's definition of "round" because the refrain lines are set to melodic phrases that are also used as part of the verse melody. His "round," in fact, describes not only the rondeaux form but also the virelai and the ballade, since all three set the refrain lines to music also used for the verses. Grocheio has grouped these three forms under the common heading "round dance" even though they have different specific formal schemes, probably because they are danced in a similar fashion—in the round. The carol, the remaining poetic form related to dance, has a somewhat different musical form and dance formation, as we shall see below.

Instrumental Dances

As with vocal dance music, the only theoretical statements about instrumental dance music exist in the treatise by Grocheio, which contains brief descriptions of three different types: ductia, estampie (stantipes), and nota. He refers to the dances and dance music popular in Paris from ca. 1300, and his information will form the basis of much of the following discussion. But for the several kinds of compositions not included by Grocheio, there is little solid material on which to build a case.

THE REPERTORY OF TEXTLESS DANCES

We can begin our discussion of the dances by attempting to match the surviving repertory with the names and descriptions that have come down to us.

ESTAMPIE

Estampie is the only dance for which we have both description and named repertory from the Middle Ages. Sixteen textless compositions from two different sources are identified as estampies: eight from the thirteenth-century French source Paris BN fonds français 844, labelled "estampies" (Nos.3–10 in this edition), and eight from the late fourteenth-century Italian manuscript London, BL Additional 29987, following the heading "Istanpitta" (Nos.14–21). The description of the form by Grocheio is ambiguous and has been the subject of a number of interpretations.[21] He makes two statements relevant to the estampie:[22]

> The parts of a ductia and stantipes are commonly called *puncta*. A *punctum* is a systematic joining together of concords making harmony in ascending and descending, having two sections alike in their beginning, differing in their end, which are usually called the close and open.[23]

> An estampie is an untexted piece, having a complicated succession of concords, determined by *puncta*. . . . Because of its complicated nature, it makes the soul of the performer and listener pay close attention . . . [the estampie form] is determined by *puncta* since it is lacking in that percussive measure which is in ductia, and [the form] is recognized [by only] the differences between its *puncta*.[24]

From these statements I have concluded that Grocheio's instrumental estampie has several double *puncta* that include a common refrain with an open and close ending, and that the *puncta* are of different lengths.[25]

All sixteen estampies agree with that description. But although the dances from the two manuscripts all conform to Grocheio's general formal description, the two sets are quite different in terms of length, meter, internal formal design, and melodic style. The French estampies have relatively short *puncta* of eight to twenty units of measure and are in triple meter, while in the Italian source they vary in length from twenty to over a hundred units of measure and are all in a basic duple division. Even more striking are the differences in formal plot and tonal orientation. Since I have described these differences elsewhere I will summarize my findings here.[26]

The two sets of estampies were composed according to different formal principles. Each *punctum* of a French estampie has completely new melodic material, followed by common open and close endings that act as its refrain, yielding a formal plot as follows (x = first or open ending, y = second or close):

Verse	Endings
A	x/y
B	x/y
C	x/y
	etc.

In contrast, the formal plots of the Italian estampies are far more complex. There are a number of formal variants, with verses containing two to four sections each and involving different combinations of sections from verse to verse. The form of "Ghaetta" (No.14) will illustrate one of the forms:

Verse	Endings
ABC	x/y
DEC	x/y
F EC	x/y
GBC	x/y

In this dance each new double *punctum* (*pars*) begins with new material, continues with a second section of either new or old material, and concludes with a refrain and open and close endings. Another, somewhat different formal combination can be seen in "Tre Fontane" (No.17), in which each *punctum* begins with a new melodic section that replaces one or more sections in the previous *punctum*, but always ends with the common refrain:

Verse	Endings
ABCD	x/y
E BCD	x/y
F CD	x/y
G D	x/y

A single refrain, as shown in these two diagrams, occurs in six of the Italian estampies, but in "Parlamento" and "In Pro" (Nos.19 and 20), there is a change of refrain and endings for the last two *puncta*. Both dances have the same form:

Verse	Endings	
AB	x/y	
CB	x/y	
DB	x/y	
EF	s/t	(new refrain and endings)
GF	s/t	

Detailed analysis of melodic and phrase construction reveals significant differences between the French and Italian estampies. The melodies of the French estampies have relatively narrow ranges and are diatonic, emphasizing a single mode. The phrases are short; and within each estampie, all the phrases are generated from a small number of melodic-rhythmic motives. In contrast, the ranges of the Italian estampies are wide, and the melodies are not modal but based on a contrast of tetrachords that include chromatic variation. The phrases are long and include a large number of melodic-rhythmic motives. That these Italian estampies bear more resemblance to dance music of the eastern Mediterranean than to European music of the same period has occurred to at least one other writer.[27] (This subject is further discussed in the section "Performance Practices," below.) In spite of the differences, the titles of the dances and their conformity to the theoretical description are assurances that they are all estampies.

Four other pieces also conform to the description of an estampie, as stated by Grocheio and illustrated by all the above compositions: two each from the Robertsbridge and Faenza codices (Nos. 43–46 in this edition). I have reconstructed the two compositions from the Faenza Codex, which in the manuscript lack all the markings necessary to provide clear division into sections. Some uncertainty remains concerning their exact forms, but a sufficient number of signs indicating repeat marks and endings survive in the manuscript to confirm that both compositions are in estampie form.[28]

The earliest surviving examples of the estampie are "Kalenda Maya" and "Souvent souspire" (Nos. 1a and 1b in this edition). It is reported that the text of "Kalenda Maya" was composed to an already existing instrumental estampie.[29] Both works are certainly estampies; the text of "Kalenda Maya" claims as much, and both works conform to the descriptions of a vocal estampie found in Grocheio and in two poetic treatises from approximately the same time.[30] But these sources also indicate that there is an essential difference between the overall forms of the vocal and the instrumental estampies that involves the position of the refrain. As described in the treatises, a vocal estampie consists of several double *puncta* (an entire stanza) and ends with a refrain. In an instrumental estampie, however, the refrain is included in each *punctum* and is repeated when the *punctum* is repeated.[31] The difference—whether the refrain is repeated only after a complete stanza or at the end of each *punctum*—is significant enough to establish the two forms as separate and to allow us to doubt the story of the origin of "Kalenda Maya." If the music did exist independently of the text it would have been in a different form. In its present form the music of both these songs well suits poems of matching stanzas with several couplets and a refrain, but in order to be an instrumental estampie additional sets of *puncta* are needed and the refrain would have to be repeated at the end of each *punctum*.

DUCTIA

The second instrumental dance described in Grocheio's treatise is the ductia:

> A ductia is also an untexted piece, measured with an appropriate percussion (*decenti percussione*). . . . But I say with regular percussion (*recta percussione*), because these beats measure it and the movement of the performer, and excite the soul of man to moving ornately according to that art they call dancing, and they [the percussive beats] measure its movements in line dance (*ductia*) and in rounds (*choreis*).[32]

Grocheio contrasts the ductia and the estampie, the most obvious difference being the "regular percussion" (*recta percussion*) of the ductia, which is missing from the estampie. This causes the estampie to be more complicated and to require more concentration. Otherwise, we learn from this and other statements by Grocheio that the ductia is similar to the estampie in having several double *puncta* and a refrain with open and close endings. Siegmund Levarie has proposed that Grocheio's remark about the estampie having a "complicated nature" refers to phrases of unequal length.[33] The use of the word "percussion" (*percussione mensuratus* and *recta percussione*) can be understood according a statement Grocheio makes earlier in the treatise that *all* sound made by instruments is percussion:

> But if all these things are considered more carefully, they are found to happen through percussion, since every sound is caused by striking, as is proven in my remarks on the soul.[34]

Therefore, the phrase about presence or absence of "appropriate percussive measure" can be interpreted as having or lacking the same number of sounds per *punctum*. Thus the difference between the two dance forms would be that the estampie has phrases of unequal length while those of the ductia are all the same length. In all other matters (refrains, repeats, etc.) the two forms are similar.

Students of Grocheio's theory have noticed that there are no surviving musical examples called "ductia." It has also been noticed, most recently by John Stevens and Christopher Page, that there are neither theoretical statements nor musical examples for what would seem to be the most commonly mentioned dance in medieval literature, the carol.[35] Both Page and I, approaching the problem from somewhat different angles, have proposed that Grocheio's ductia is in fact the carol.[36] The name "ductia" was probably chosen by Grocheio to describe the essential aspect of the dance formation, namely, that it took several different shapes (round, line, etc.—at the whim of its leader [*ductia*, from *duco*, leader]) and because the several meanings of the Latin word for carol, "choreis," would confuse the description of this dance with that of the vocal dance "round" (*rotundellus*), discussed above, a dance performed entirely in the round formation.[37]

Although no compositions come down to us with the label "ductia," nor do we have any thirteenth- or fourteenth-century carols with music, I have made a tentative identification of the two forms by comparing Grocheio's description of the vocal ductia to that of the earliest carol repertory from fifteenth-century English sources.[38] In any case, Grocheio's description of the instrumental ductia, regardless of its possible association with the carol, is that it has even-length double *puncta*, a refrain, and open and close endings. Three of the dances from Paris, BN 844 (Nos.11–13 in this edition) would seem to fit that description. (In the manuscript No.11 is marked "dansse real"; No.12 is untitled; and No.13 is labeled "danse.")[39]

NOTA

Grocheio makes only a passing reference to a third instrumental dance form, the nota. He describes it as having four double *puncta* and remarks that it could be considered "either a form of ductia or an incomplete estampie."[40]

In the lines from Jehan Maillart quoted above a distinction is made between estampies, dances, and notas (*estempies, Danses, noctes et baleriez*). Although this does not add to what Grocheio has told us, it confirms the fact that the nota was a separate form. The only other use of the term known to me is from the tenth-century writings of Regino of Prum, in which the word "nothae" is assigned to antiphons that do not conform to a single mode.[41] Only two surviving compositions are identified as notas; both are texted, and the only thing they have in common is that both have some elements of estampie and ductia while not conforming exactly to either form.[42] One can speculate from this small amount of evidence that the form of a nota was, as Grocheio states, a dance piece with some aspects of estampie and ductia, i.e., at least some double *puncta* and perhaps a refrain, but in some way different from both.

Four comparisons seem to answer this description: the three from BL Harley 978 (Nos.39–41 in this edition) and one from Oxford, Bodleian Library, MS Douce 139 (No.2). In the pieces from Harley 978, the *puncta* are written out rather than marked for repeat, as in estampies and ductias; and the composer took advantage of the polyphonic aspect of the pieces to present somewhat different methods of repeating and varying the phrases: No.39 is composed of three melodic phrases that are repeated in the lower voice to a continually changing counterpoint in the upper voice; No.40 has two phrases, presented first in the lower voice, then repeated in the upper voice, transposed up a fifth; and No.41 has only a single melodic phrase, presented twice in the lower voice and three times in the upper voice, transposed up a fifth. The formal plots are as follows (ctpt = counterpoint):

No. 39

Section	1	2	3	4	5	6
Upper voice	ctpt 1	ctpt2	ctpt3	ctpt4	ctpt5	ctpt6
Lower voice	A	B	C	A	B	C

No. 40

Section	1	2	3	4
Upper voice	ctpt1	ctpt2	A	B
Lower voice	A	B	ctpt3	ctpt4

No. 41

Section	1	2	3	4	5
Upper voice	ctpt1	ctpt2	A	A	A
Lower voice	A	A	ctpt3	ctpt4	ctpt5

In all three dances each *punctum* is heard twice, although not in succession, as in the dances discussed earlier. No.41 is merely a single *punctum* performed five times, each time with new counterpoint, somewhat like a theme and variations except that the variations consist of four counterpoints and, for the fifth phrase, embellishment of the melody itself.

If we accept "nota" as a catchall word for dance compositions with unique forms, these three instrumental pieces can be seen as "a kind of ductia"—that is, having regular phrases; or "an incomplete estampie"—that is, without the refrain. But since Grocheio tells us that refrains are a part of all dances, we may conclude either that these are not dances or that there was a type of English dance without refrain that was unknown to Grocheio.

The fourth possible nota is also somewhat of a puzzle. Oxford, Douce 139 (No.2) has ten versicles, more than any other known dance; some are clearly marked for repeat, some have written-out repeats, and some are possibly without repeats. It is the only medieval instrumental composition known that is monophonic for most of its length and has a single polyphonic section (or more correctly, a section of expanded monophony). The irregular length of the *puncta* gives this composition some resemblance to the estampies already seen, but the apparent absence of a refrain eliminates it from being exactly in that form. It is possible that the composition is merely a succession of *puncta*, some totally unrelated to one another, ending with a polyphonic versicle. This is the form in which the composition is usually edited, as it is here. There is so little relationship between beginning and end that Jacques Handschin has speculated that it may be two different estampies.[43] The compositions most closely related to this format of a succession of *puncta* without refrain are the two texted notas described above.

Another possibility is that the clue to the order of the *puncta* is provided by the appearance of the manuscript page.[44] The polyphonic *punctum* is placed in the center of the page with most of the *puncta* above it, a misplaced half-*punctum* next to it on the left, and another misplaced half-*punctum* on the right. The unusual placement of the polyphonic *punctum*, and indeed the very existence of a polyphonic *punctum* in an otherwise monophonic composition, may mean that the polyphonic section is a refrain, to be played after every double *punctum* in the piece. The evidence for this is certainly very weak, and I put it forward only as a possibility. If each *punctum* were to be repeated (i.e., double *puncta* throughout) and the polyphonic *punctum* were to be played after each one, this composition would fit the description of an estampie. Without the refrain the only dance description it resembles is that of the nota.

OTHER DANCES

Several compositions are found in the repertory with dance names that are not described by Grocheio or by any other theorist. They can only be treated by describing what is evident in the music itself.

Saltarello

Four dances survive in MS BL 29987 with the name "salterello" (*sic*) (Nos.22–25), a word known to be associated with dancing as early as the fifteenth century.[45] Literary references and dance treatises indicate that it was a very lively dance, consistent with the derivation of the name from *saltare*, to jump. These saltarellos are similar in formal design to the estampies in the same manuscript, although there is quite a bit of variety in their compositional technique. They vary in length from quite short (No. 24) to the extreme length of the Italian estampies. The longest, No.22, has formal and melodic properties similar to those of the estampies. Saltarellos Nos.23 and 24 also have complex formal details, but their melodic phrases are short and are more closely oriented toward the Western techniques of a minimum number of melodic-rhythmic motives with few chromatics. The form of No.25 is unique; similar to the estampies, it consists of a basic refrain preceded by different introductory phrases, but the introductory phrases are not self-contained. Each beginning phrase consists of only two or four measures, and in verses 3–6 each new phrase is added to the preceding one, producing the following form:

Verse	Ending
AB	x/y
B	x/y
CB	x/y
DCB	x/y
EDCB	x/y
FEDCB	x/y

The saltarellos present a wider variation in overall length and complexity of formal design than do the Italian estampies. The basic formal elements are common to both sets of dances, however, indicating that the major difference between saltarello and estampie must have been the dance steps not the musical form (see Dance Pairs, below).

Dance Pairs and Trotto

The three dance pairs (Nos.26, 27, and 29) have several characteristics in common: The first of each pair has a title—"Lamento di Tristano" (No.26), "La Manfredina" (No.27), and "Dança Amorosa" (No.29); the afterdance—called "rotta" in Nos.27 and 28, and "troto" in No.29—derives its melody from the titled dance; and the phrases in the afterdances are shorter and in smaller note values than those of the title dances. All the members of the dance pairs have three relatively short double *puncta* of irregular lengths, thus relating them in form to the estampie and the saltarello.[46] The titles may refer to particular dance choreographies, similar to those found in the fifteenth-century bassadanze and balli (see below). A tempting connection in this regard can be found for "Dança Amorosa," in that a ballo choreography entitled "Amoroso" is found in three fifteenth-century Italian dance manuals. Music is included in one of those sources, but it does not resemble the dance included here.[47]

One meaning of the word "rotta" is a route, or a path[48] and if that is its meaning here it probably refers to the dance steps and formation (suggesting a possible connection between rotta and carol steps, although the musical forms are different).[49] The fact that the dances are paired may indicate that they functioned as slow-fast pairs, similar to the standard pairing in the sixteenth century. The usual set was a stately dance followed by a quicker and more lively afterdance, e.g., pavane and galliard.[50] But any idea of a standard pairing in this fourteenth-century repertory is complicated by the third dance pair (No.29), which has a "troto" rather than a "rotta" as the afterdance, and by the existence of an independent and unpaired "Trotto" (No.28). "Trotto" and "troto" would seem to be variations of the same word, and both are probably derived from *trottare*, to trot. The two dances are alike in formal and melodic style, and in both aspects they resemble the short saltarellos. They have irregular-length phrases, four versicles (but probably originally five) in Trotto, No.28, and three in Troto, No.29.

It is tempting to try to reconcile these dances, which have similar musical characteristics and names. Since the dance pairs are from two different manuscripts, it is possible that "troto" and "rotta" may have been interchangeable as descriptions of this type of afterdance (i.e. "rotta," in a line; and "troto,"—trotted). With so few examples it is difficult to come to any clear conclusions, but I present the following two speculations: First, that the words "trotto," "troto," and "rotta" may be different ways to describe the same dance, and we are lacking the titled first dance for which the "trotto" (No.28) is an afterdance. On the other hand, "trotto" ("troto") and "rotta" may be different dances, but either type could be used as an afterdance. I am inclined more toward the first conclusion because the melody of the "troto" is derived from its preceding dance in the same way as those of the two "rottas." In his early fifteenth-century dance instructions, Domenico da Piacenza provides information on how one may perform a saltarello to bassadanza music,[51] indicating that there was by that time a tradition of deriving one dance from the music for another. All three titled dances with their afterdances would seem to be examples of an early form of that tradition. Although little else is known about dance pairs until the sixteenth century, the existence of these three sets in Italian sources, with a date earlier than 1390 certain for "Dança Amorosa," indicates that the custom was more than fifty years old by the time Domenico mentions it.

Unidentified Dances

The remainder of the pieces included in this collection are less securely associated with dance. With the exception of "Bel fiore dança," they are with-

out dance titles or other indications that were linked with dancing at any time.
This lack of direct word association does not necessarily indicate that the pieces
cannot be dances, and indeed several of them contain the kinds of musical
phrases (i.e., rhythmic patterns and regular meter) that make identification
as dances quite possible. Others, however, can be related only vaguely with
the more secure dance compositions.

"Bel fiore dança"

"Bel fiore dança" (No.47) calls itself a dance, although it does not resemble
any known dance from the period. It is in two unequal *partes* with no indication
of repeats, but it is possible that it is incomplete and was intended to have
several *puncta* and refrains, which would relate it to all the dances discussed
above; the confused state of the notation for the other two dances in this
manuscript (Nos.45 and 46) makes that a distinct possibility. There is, however, another more interesting possibility: that the dance is a correct and
complete version of a bassadanza.

The definitive history of dance and dance music in the early fifteenth century has yet to be written, but we do know that by the mid-fifteenth century
there were two related court dances in Italy—bassadanza and ballo.[52] The
bassadanza was related to the French basse danse, a slow-moving dance with
an elegant series of low step movements (*bassa*, low to the floor). The ballo,
however, was made up of different kinds of steps, including the jumping steps
of the saltarello, and had four *misure* (similar to tempo): in order of speed
from the slowest motion, these were bassadanza, quadernaria, saltarello, and
piva.[53] Several treatises on Italian courtly dancing survive from the fifteenth
century or slightly later,[54] and eight of them list a ballo—but not a bassadanza—named "Belfiore." The music for balli and bassadanze exists only as
tenor lines, and in the one source in which the tenor for the ballo "Belfiore"
is included, it bears only a distant resemblance to the lower line of "Bel fiore
dança." But there is a possibility that the two dances were related on another
level, that of dedication to the same patron. "Belfiore" was the name given to
the palace constructed in 1390–1392 in Ferrara for Nicolò III, and there is
evidence that the ballo "Belfiore" in the dance treatise was written for and at
Nicolò's court.[55] "Bel fiore dança" could not be a ballo because it lacks the
mixture of meters associated with that dance form, but it could be a bassadanza. Its lower line is similar in shape and length to all existing bassadanza
tenors known from slightly later in the fifteenth century,[56] for example, to
the well-known polyphonic bassadanza "La Spagna."[57] If the identification of
"Bel fiore dança" is correct, it is the earliest-known example of a bassadanza.

"Chançoneta Tedescha"

The four bass melodies named "Chançoneta Tedescha" and "Chançona
Tedescha" (Nos.35–38) resemble the known basse danse tenors mentioned
above in that they are all in two *partes* and are written in black breves and
semibreves. It is interesting to note that the Italian manuscript names them
"German songs," suggesting that this type of dance—or perhaps this particular

form of the tenor—was considered to be of German origin. In some of the fifteenth-century Italian dance manuals there is a step called *saltarello todesco*, meaning a saltarello step danced in the somewhat slower *quadernaria misura*.[58] There is no way to know if this is what is meant by the titles of the "Chançonete Tedesca." The influx of German instrumentalists into Italy beginning early in the fifteenth century is well documented and thus would be one obvious source of this material.[59] In actual performance the tenor notes of the basse danse would have been played by one instrumentalist while one or two others would have improvised to it.[60] The basse danse steps presently known are all from Italy and France, and outside of the *saltarello todesco*, nothing is known of what would have been the German practice for this kind of dance in the early fifteenth century.

"Czaldy Waldy"

The two compositions included here under the title "Czaldy Waldy" (No.30) may or may not have been intended to function as a pair—if in fact either of them is a dance.[61] Both have two *partes* and are written in black notes, thus conforming to the basic format of the basse danse as discussed above, and therefore it is possible that these pieces are the Czech equivalent of that dance form. The name "Czaldy Waldy" appears in just one of the two manuscripts and only at the beginning of the second of the two compositions; in the concordant manuscript, which includes only the second piece, there is no name at all.

"Chose Tassin"

The three tenors marked "Chose Tassin" (Nos.31–33) have been included here on the strength of the reference in Grocheio that a performer named Tassinus performed difficult estampies of seven *puncta*.[62] "Chose Loyset" (No.34) is included by extension, on the grounds that the "chose" of "Chose Tassin" may indicate that it is (or was) a dance. All four compositions appear in the same source, where they serve as tenors to three-part motets.[63] They probably were not dances in the form we find them here, but it is possible that they were originally dance melodies or dance tenors that were chosen as raw material for the motets. The three pieces entitled "Chose Tassin" are in reality written-out double *puncta* with open and close endings. "Chose Loyset" is marked off in the manuscript in three sections, but actually the same melodic figure is written out six times. In these formats the pieces do not seem to possess the regularity of rhythm usually associated with the other dance melodies or dance tenors included in this publication, but that may not necessarily exclude them from the category of medieval dance.

No.42

No.42, a third composition from the Robertsbridge Codex, is included here only because it appears in the manuscript immediately before No.43; for that reason alone, it has always been assumed to be another estampie-type dance. There is reason to doubt that it is a dance—or at least an estampie—because of the format of the surviving fragment. In most other estampies, including the two in this manuscript, the complete open and close endings are given in full at the end of the first *punctum* and indicated only by sign after all subsequent *puncta*. Thus, if the opening section were lost we would have only the beginnings of the remaining *puncta* and a cue to repeat the refrain and endings (as in the incomplete No.3, from manuscript 844). In this fragment, however, although only the end of the composition survives, it contains a complete pair of open and close endings. There is not enough here to allow further speculation as to the piece's actual form or function.

SUMMARY

The repertory of supposed medieval instrumental dances, therefore, consists of a small, disparate collection of compositions and fragments. They can be broken down by national origin and type, as shown in Table 1.[64]

Table 1

	France	Italy	England	Czechoslovakia	Totals
Estampies	8	10	2		20
Carols	3				3
Saltarellos		4			4
Trottos		1			1
Dance pairs		3			3
Tenors	4	4		2	10
Notas			4		4
Bassadanzas		1			1
Totals	15	23	6	2	46

Even with the inclusion of some questionable compositions, the total number of dances is extremely small in view of the popularity of dancing in Europe in the late Middle Ages. On the other hand, since few instrumental musicians of the time could read or write music (or anything else for that matter), we should perhaps wonder why any of this repertory has survived at all. Several theories have been put forward to explain the existence of these pieces, including their possible use as didactic literature[65] and their derivation from a foreign style.[66] In any case, the quantity is so small that it provides only a tiny glimpse of what must have been a major musical repertory. And since each nation developed its own dancing traditions, the total number of dances from any one country is far too small to allow more than a start at refining our knowledge according to national styles. Some of the peculiarities of the various compositions have been pointed out above—e.g., the differences between the structure of French and Italian estampies—but there are too many unknowns to speculate much further along those lines. For the present we can only observe the similarities and differences in the few surviving compositions and attempt to relate the music to the rest of the picture of dancing in the Middle Ages.

ANCING

By calling upon all the information at our disposal, it is now possible to speculate a bit about the general nature of the dances that were accompanied by the music in this volume.

ROUND AND CAROL

The very names "round" and "carol" furnish some idea of these two dances. Both were danced in a group and involved a formation in the round for at least part of the dance. In the Siena and Florence frescoes (Plates 1 and 2), the dancers' feet are shown close to the ground; the artists have suggested graceful motions rather than vigorous leaping steps. In both works the circle is broken, suggesting that the round formation is only a basic position from which other formations proceed. In the Siena fresco the dancers are threading their way under a "bridge" formed by two dancers with hands joined; and in the Florence work there are two formations: a closed circle of four dancers and a line of three, each group holding hands. The music for the dancers in both scenes is provided by a lone tambourine player standing in their midst, her mouth open, presumably singing the carol verse, to which the dancers would join in singing the refrain. This conforms to the passage from Boccaccio quoted earlier, and even more closely to the French practice as described by Maillart:

> Then the napery was taken up, and when they had washed their hands, the carols began. Those ladies who had sweet voices sang loudly: everyone answered them joyfully, anyone who knew how to sing, sang thus:[67]

The two dances, round and carol, were apparently danced to quite different tempi. Grocheio tells us the round is "sung in a slow rhythm" and the carol (ductia) is "rapid in its ascent and descent."[68] But there may have been some variation from country to country, since Boccaccio states that the carol step was danced "with slow steps" (see quotation above), and Chaucer describes it as involving turns and springing steps:

> Tho mightest thou karolles sene,
> And folke daunce and mery bene,
> And make many a fayre tournyng
> Vpon the grene grasse springyng.[69]

Chaucer also tells of a couple who had the opportunity to kiss as they danced the carol; this suggests that at one point in the dance the couples paired off:

> And fayre tressed euery tresse,
> Had Myrthe done, for his noblesse,
> Amydde the carole for to daunce;
> But herof lyeth no remembraunce,
> Howe that they daunsed queyntly:
> That one wolde come al priuely
> Agayne that other; and whan they were
> Togyther almoste, they threwe yfere
> Her mouthes so, that through her play
> It semed as they kyste alway;[70]

I would now speculate even further about the method of dancing the carol from my interpretation of Grocheio's name for it: "leader's dance." The term may refer to the dance leader as conductor of the dance formations, in line or in the round according to his whim, thus the "under-the-bridge" formation in the Siena fresco. In this connection there is documentation for at least one carol in a long line: "Such a carol had never been seen, nearly a quarter league long."[71] It would seem to follow, therefore, that if the carol involved a fairly diverse set of formations and activities, the round dance by contrast was merely danced in the round with no other formation.

ESTAMPIE

Perhaps we can gain some idea of the general nature of the estampie by examining the way it is contrasted with other dances. Many of the literary references to carol suggest a distinction between "dance" and "carol," as in Chaucer: "Festes, instrumentez, caroles, daunces, lust and array, and all the circumstances of love"[72] and Froissart: "Even before I was twelve I was greedy to see dances and carols, to hear minstrels and stories."[73] Froissart also makes the same kind of distinction between estampie and carol: "And as soon as [the minstrels] had stopped the estampies that they beat, those men and women who amused themselves dancing, without hesitation, began to take hands for carolling."[74]

The distinction between carol and dance, carol and estampie is somewhat clouded by the very nature of poetry and the poet's desire to conjure up images rather than to give technical information. Indeed, the distinction is not always made; "carol" and "dance" are often found as synonyms. But

Grocheio too suggests that there is an essential difference between the formation for the estampie and that for the round and the carol when he mentions dancing "in carol" for round and ductia, but not for estampie. Estampie, therefore, is probably the other major dance formation—couples.

As for the kinds of steps used in the estampie, its Latin name provides a major clue: *stante pedes*, standing/stationary feet,[75] suggests very little motion. Grocheio tells us that the estampie was more suitable for all ages than the energetic carol, but that it required irregular and complicated movements.

The treatises and records of the much better documented fifteenth and early sixteenth centuries may be of use in filling in the large missing sections in the above picture. Although the study of later forms will not provide exact details concerning the earlier dances, that information does tend to reinforce the sketchy earlier material and to support the conclusions about some of the early dances.

Renaissance dances in all the European countries appear to be of two general kinds: generic, i.e., composed of a standard sequence of movements that allowed the steps to be danced to any tune; and those to which specific choreographies were assigned, e.g., ballo, bassadanza, and the basse danses that had titles.[76]

The dances without special choreographies were known only by their generic names: saltarello, untitled basse danses, hoftanz, etc. This type could be danced to any music of the right tempo and meter; the dancers repeated a single sequence until the music ended. Some of the generic dances continued to be called by the same names they had in the late Middle Ages, e.g., saltarello. We do not know if the steps remained the same, but during the Renaissance the saltarello, for example, was clearly a jumping step (as its name implies), and there is no reason to believe it was not that kind of dance in earlier centuries. By extension, this continuity of type of step can be suspected of the other dances that kept their names in the later century.

Some dances changed names as they evolved, e.g., the "carol" apparently became the "farandole" and the "branle,"[77] both of which are line dances. Although some details of the steps probably changed, the later dances do provide an idea of the nature of their medieval ancestor, supporting the conclusions made above about the nature of the carol. This kind of continuity is also true of the fifteenth-century Italian bassadanza and Burgundian basse danse, which led eventually to the stately Renaissance pavan.[78] In fact, this evolution can be traced in detail from the instructions for early-Renaissance bassadanze and basse danses to those for the late-Renaissance pavan. While some of the movements and steps changed, the basic stately attitude of the dance remained intact. But where did the fifteenth-century bassadanza/basse danse come from?

The only stately dance in the late Middle Ages identified above is the estampie, which seems to have disappeared after the first few decades of the fifteenth century, just at the time that the bassadanza is found for the first time. It is unlikely that a dance as popular as the estampie would suddenly disappear without a trace and that a completely new dance of the same general attitude would originate without medieval antecedents; the history of music usually records more gradual transformations from one form to the next.

The connection between estampie and the early bassadanza is suggested here because of the similarity of the descriptions—stately and low; Ingrid Brainard describes the bassadanza as a "processional type" of dance.[79] The suspicion arises, therefore, that somewhere around the year 1400 the new bassadanza took the place of the old estampie, retaining the general characteristics of the older step, i.e., couples in stately procession, but perhaps more stylized (or perhaps only the name was changed, by the dancing masters).[80]

The choreographed dances of the early Renaissance were identified by specific titles, e.g., "La Spagna," "Roti boull joyeux," etc., so that the dancers could assign the correct step sequence. Each bassadanza and basse danse had a unique choreography that required a particular sequence of steps, but it could be danced to any tune of the correct length since the rhythm and the tempo of all these dances were the same throughout. The balli, however, had not only individual steps but also specific music, since they changed from one *misura* to another in a specific order. Their steps were combinations of the generic types.[81] They were miniature dance-dramas, acting out little scenes, and were popular as court entertainment until well into the seventeenth century.

In the estampie repertory the French pieces are called simply "estampie," whereas the Italian dances are individually named. It is possible that the Italian estampie was related to its successors, the bassadanza and the ballo, in that it was individually choreographed—thus the reason for the fanciful titles. If so, then the French estampies were probably of the generic, unchoreographed type.

These suggestions are admittedly highly speculative. They are an attempt to draw some conclusions about medieval dancing from the few clues that have survived. About the actual steps and movements we will probably never know much more than this, but for anyone wishing to reconstruct medieval dances, the following sources may help in approximating the medieval steps: For the round and line dances, the ferandole and branle steps of the later centuries, and the steps of traditional "line" folk dances, which are also probably related; for the couples dances, the steps described in the fifteenth-century basse danse and bassadanza manuals are probably very close to the medieval steps, although they became more stylized by the later dancing masters.

PERFORMANCE PRACTICES

Our knowledge of medieval instrumental performance practices is as incomplete as our information on the dance music. There is some help from literary sources and iconography in identifying the instruments used, and there exist a few theoretical statements and some ornamented intabulations of vocal works from which general principles of approach can be extracted. But for many of the most essential practical aspects of performance, there are no medieval sources of information. Speculations about practical matters can be derived from European folk music practices and from the performance of cultured music in societies of the Mediterranean area. Those practices appear to be timeless, although they have probably been influenced to some extent by other music throughout the intervening seven hundred years and therefore present a modified example of medieval practices. But they do have the advantage of being a living musical tradition, and when those practices seem to agree with historical information they can be useful in providing practical models. In any case, whatever their shortcomings, they are our closest link to the lost tradition we wish to recreate in the performance of the surviving medieval dance repertory.

This repertory is not unified and cannot be considered evidence of a single performance practice. In recent years musicologists have studied several of these compositions and have suggested methods of performance. At the basis of most of these investigations and hypotheses is the question of why any of this material survives at all. By rights no medieval dance repertory should have been written down, and recent studies assume that the survival of the few existing compositions is due to some very special characteristics or circumstances.

Ewald Jammers has demonstrated through an analysis of "Ghaetta" and "Isabella," from MS BL 29987, that the estampies from that manuscript can be reduced to embellishments of a relatively sustained basic melody.[82] Following a similar technique of reduction, both Kenneth Zuckerman and I have noted that the sustained basic melodic notes in these estampies produce scale patterns related to Eastern melodic traditions, thus aligning them more closely with the ragas of the East than with the European modes.[83] The melody of "Ghaetta" illustrates the point made in greater detail in those studies.

The phrases of "Ghaetta" (No.14) appear to be melodic and rhythmic decorations of a set of individual pitches. In the first section, for example, the melody stays mostly within the range of the tetrachord *b* to *f*, concentrating on decorations of first *d*, then *e* and *c*, and finally *f*. The next section, ending at the refrain, presents decorations of the descending tetrachord *b♭*, *a*, *g*, and *f♯*. The refrain, up to and including both endings, explores the relationship of the various notes of the two earlier tetrachords, using both *b* and *b♭*. The two principal notes of the entire *prima pars*, according to rhythmic emphasis and melodic placement, are *d* and *g*. Similar analysis of the remainder of the composition supports the conclusion that the entire dance consists of melodic-rhythmic elaborations of the scale from *f♯* to high *f*, with a final on *g* and a dominant on *d*.

Composition by means of an elaboration of the notes of contrasting tetrachords was not a European technique in the late Middle Ages, but it was and still is common in the music of the eastern Mediterranean countries. Jacques Handschin noted in 1929 that there was much similarity between these dance forms and the traditional eastern Mediterranean composition known as *peşrev*.[84] From this similarity I have concluded that the Italian estampies conform more to the Turkish *makam* system[85] and Arabic theoretical practices[86] than to the techniques of Western Europe. This relationship supports adoption of some of the performance practices in the traditional music of the eastern Mediterranean countries for part of the present repertory, as will be proposed below.

In recent publications Wulf Arlt has theorized that some of the dances could have been illustrations of compositional or improvisational techniques.[87] He finds in several of the compositions in the present edition evidence of the process of elaboration of simple melodic cells and, in the case of the polyphonic examples, of varieties of contrapuntal lines that can be written. In the dance from MS Douce 139 (No.2), for example, he notes that sections 2 and 3 consist of different introductions built onto the melody of section 1. And from observations of similar kinds of elaboration patterns in other dances, he concludes that many of them could have been written as pedagogical tools to demonstrate textless compositional techniques.

Neither of the above theories can be proven, but regardless of the accuracy of the conclusions, the details of musical construction brought out in the analyses do suggest possibilities for the performance of this repertory. The point has been made by many scholars that the medieval concept of a melody was closer to that of a filled-in outline than it was to something given an immutable form by its composer, and it can be seen from the analyses that this concept holds true for the present repertory. When placed in conjunction with the evidence presented below concerning the method of elaborating a melodic line, definite ideas emerge as to how one may approach these compositions in performance.

INSTRUMENTS

Although we can learn about the use of specific musical instruments from medieval literary sources and iconographic representations, care must be taken because of the nature of the information. Poetic/artistic license is always present to varying degrees, and the writers and painters assumed that their audience would be well aware of current performance practices, thus allowing additional poetic leeway and lack of historical precision. For example, the following passages from the mid-fourteenth-century "Remède de Fortune" by Guillaume de Machaut list a large number of musical instruments in association with dancing:

> But you should have seen after the meal
> The minstrels who entered in generous number,
> With shining hair and simple dress!
> They played many varied harmonies.
> For I saw there all in a group
> Vielle, rebec, gittern,
> [13 additional lines of instruments]
> And certainly, it seems to me
> That never was such melody
> Seen nor heard,
> For each of them, according to the tone
> Of his instrument, without discord,
> Plays on vielle, gittern, citole,
> Harp, trumpet, horn, flageolet,
> Pipe, bellows, bagpipe, nakers,
> Or tabor, and every sound that one can make
> With fingers, quill and bow
> I heard and saw in that park.
> When they had finished an estampie,
> The ladies and their friends
> Went off in twos and threes,
> Holding one another by the hand,
> To a very beautiful chamber;[88]

Machaut tells us that all instruments one can finger, pluck, and bow could be used in the performance of dance music; but he does not say that they were all equally good choices for all kinds of dances. Although the poet does not mention it, we know from other evidence that it is unlikely that all the instruments listed would have been played at the same time; and indeed there is no implication in the poem that a single ensemble is being described. But we do not know whether, or to what extent, certain instruments might have been considered appropriate only for specific types of dances and not for others. A perusal of several literary sources yields a list of instruments found in the company of dancing that includes virtually all instruments known to have existed at the time. But, as in the poem, the information is unrefined and leaves numerous questions unanswered.

It is possible to limit somewhat the list of instruments. Above all others, the one most frequently mentioned as performing for dances, especially for the estampie, is the vielle. This is true in the literature of France, England, Italy, Germany, and the Low Countries.[89] Grocheio states that the vielle is the ideal instrument for all secular music.[90] Vielle players are mentioned performing alone, in pairs, and, in one account, in four: "Then the servants hurried and quickly took away the napery. Four minstrels of the vielle played a new estampie before the lady."[91]

Inconographic sources augment our information in terms of viable instruments and ensembles. We can find illustrations of nearly all the instruments mentioned in Machaut's poem. Solo instruments most frequently depicted with dancers include the vielle (and rebec), plucked strings of various sizes and shapes, the harp, the bagpipe, the shawm (or similar wind instrument), and the tambourine (with vocal dances). The ensembles shown often consist of two or more vielles, two lutes, lute and harp, pipe and tabor (single player or two players), and a shawm band—two or three shawms with trombone (slide trumpet?).

Unfortunately, as with literary sources, iconography does not tell us which instruments were associated with what repertory. It is not even clear that there was a difference in the choice of instruments between rustic (peasant) and courtly scenes. A close survey of the evidence has yet to be done, but a preliminary look shows very little class distinction in instrument use. Further, we do not know if there was a significant difference in the dance repertory for the two social strata. Did they have entirely different types of dance music? Or, if they shared musical types, was the round dance of the peasant musically different in either form or melodic content from that of the upper class? And if there was a difference in the repertory (rather than in just the instrument selection), are the surviving musical examples presented here only representative of the courtly tradition, thus suggesting that we should ignore the sources of information that are clearly of peasant reference?

Nevertheless, leaving these unanswered (and for the present time unanswerable) questions as a caution to the reader, one can reach the broad conclusion that nearly every instrument of the time can be safely associated with dance music, and therefore the modern performer need only be careful about the time period and geographical popularity of specific instruments.[92]

TEMPO

Tempo is a difficult problem in all early music. Lacking modern timepieces, the early performers used the normal heartbeat as a basic pulse (60–80 beats per minute), and then varied the notation to adjust the tempo of each composition. Tempo, therefore, is related to the actual notation itself; and the incipit provided with each transcription in this edition can help the performer in understanding the tempo and metric organization of the composition. Although the method of ascertaining tempo remained constant during the period covered by these compositions, the note (or notes) to which the counting unit was assigned was not always the same, differing according to date, the particulars of mensuration (duple or triple subdivision), and national tradition.[93] To assist the performer I have indicated in the Critical Notes what I believe to be the counting unit. Most of the pieces are uncomplicated, so that once the initial pace has been set the entire dance proceeds with no change in the relationship of the written note to the beat. In the few compositions in which the ratio changes within the piece, editorial markings relate new sections to old. The reader is encouraged to study the sources and come to a personal conclusion concerning the tempi of these compositions. The heartbeat tempo of 60–80 beats per minute is fairly general and allows a margin of choice to the performer, as is true of most of the other aspects of performance. The final selection of tempo should be adjusted to the musical demands of the individual melodic lines and to the particular performance conditions, such as the actual instruments (their types and number), the quantity of ornamentation employed, and acoustical considerations.

ORNAMENTATION AND IMPROVISATION

Information for the elaboration of a melody can be found in a theoretical treatise, in the survival of variant versions of some compositions, and in two manuscripts that include ornamented instrumental versions of vocal compositions.

Theoretical Evidence

The theoretical information is provided by Jerome of Moravia (Paris, late thirteenth century, a contemporary of Grocheio). His comments on ornamentation appear in a chapter entitled "The Method of Singing and Making Notes and Rests in Ecclesiastical Song," but they are directed toward both vocal and instrumental performance and can serve for secular as well as sacred music.[94] Although Jerome's statements have been published in translation, there is no modern commentary on that information. What follows, therefore, is my summary of his procedures of melodic ornamentation:

1. Interruption or separation of conjunct notes by use of quick glottal stops, a practice Jerome refers to as "breathing," is an ornament intended mostly for vocal performance.

2. "Reverberation" is a category of ornament that includes an extremely rapid anticipation before a written pitch (modern appoggiatura) at the interval of a tone or a semitone; the separation of a given note into two or more notes of the same pitch; and the use of (in modern terms) both the mordent and the trill at the interval of a semitone, a tone, or some other interval (Jerome does not elaborate on which other intervals would be appropriate). When describing the subdivision of a pitch Jerome makes special mention of the use of triple as well as duple subdivision.

3. Another version of appoggiatura he calls "stormy note," a rising semitone

that is sung unhurriedly and is not articulated separately from the pitch it embellishes.

4. The longest and most detailed description is of the trill (also perhaps vibrato[95]), which Jerome calls "harmonic flower" (*flos harmonicus*). He advocates its use by both voice and instrument. In this category he first describes a quick mordent, which he refers to as a swift and stormlike vibration. He also describes a "long" trill, with steady vibrations that do not exceed a semitone, and an "open" trill, which is also steady and does not exceed a whole tone.

5. Within the trill category he also includes the "sudden" ornament, a trill of a semitone that begins with steady vibration and increases in speed. In reference to the organ, his instrumental example, Jerome could only be referring to a trill because of the technical limitations of the instrument. But for vocal music the statement could also mean that the interval itself increases from a very small one to a semitone—he says it should not exceed a semitone—along with the increasing speed of the beats. In modern notation this ornament might be expressed as ∿∿. When a trill is performed on an organ, Jerome tells us, the main note is held down while the key above it is pressed and released. This, of course, would result in the sounding of both notes each time the higher key is depressed.

Jerome's treatise also offers a bit of assistance with the placement of ornaments:

1. Ornaments should not be used on any note smaller than the semibreve, and the "reverberation" (appoggiatura, subdivision, mordent, trill) is restricted to notes longer than the semibreve; that is, they can be applied only to the breve and the longa. The semibreve was the equivalent of the modern "counting note," i.e., a quarter note in 4/4 meter.

2. Ornaments are to be placed only on the unaltered notes of the mode. I conclude here that Jerome considers non-modal notes (accidentals, or other notes outside the limits of the normal modal range) to be ornaments themselves and so should not be further ornamented.

3. The "long" trill is usually restricted to the initial note of the phrase and to the penultimate and final notes of the mode when the interval of a rising semitone is involved. The first part of this rule is clear as stated. The second section can be interpreted to mean that a sustained, even trill is to be used only at those cadence points involving the final of the mode, when the final is approached from a half-step below. What will result is a half-tone trill on the penultimate note. It will involve the pitch of the final, thus anticipating the sounding of the final and making a graceful phrase ending. It is important to note that the use of this ornament—the gentlest of those Jerome describes—is restricted to places where it will heighten the feeling of the cadence.

4. In his discussion of the use of trills in cadences, after describing the ascending half-step cadence and the "long" trill, Jerome makes the rather obscure statement "but if certain other manners are established in descending, the second note of the syllable should have an open embellishment." I interpret this to mean that if the phrase ends by descent to the final, an "open" trill

can be used, the specific interval of the trill—up to a whole tone—depending on the natural intervals of the mode itself.

5. In the "sudden embellishment," Jerome states that "short notes are placed for the beauty of the harmony." This seems to advocate the use of a turn or some such method of ending this ornament gracefully.

6. An appoggiatura is permitted at the beginning of all ornaments, at the interval of a tone or a semitone for any pitch of the scale except the final. Before the final it must always be a semitone, but in that position it can also be sung as a "stormy note." Jerome also tells us that the "stormy note" is a French technique used in "certain songs, though not in all." He seems to be referring to the emotional nature of this ornament, which makes it inappropriate in certain kinds of songs (pastorals, for example).

In summary, Jerome appears to advocate many of the vocal and instrumental ornamental practices associated with performance of the music of the eastern Mediterranean countries, thus providing additional weight to the recent theories mentioned above.

Verification that ornamentation and variation were basic ingredients of medieval performance practice can be deduced from a comparison of concordant manuscript versions of many medieval compositions. Although the dance repertory cannot be used to demonstrate this point because all but two are unique copies, any number of examples can be drawn from the vocal repertory.[96] An analysis of the variants shows that medieval musicians thought it necessary to retain specific structural elements and characteristic melodic motives of each composition but at the same time felt free to make both rhythmic and melodic alterations. A typical medieval performance was probably a personal version built around a composition's most essential elements, filled in with spontaneous embellishments and variations by the performer(s).[97] A reflection of the spirit of this tradition can be found in the literature of the Middle Ages, which exhibits similar variant transmissions of stories and narratives; it was obviously considered the right and duty of any transmitter of tales to add, vary, and embellish the stories according to his own inspiration. In some cases the essential ingredients of the traditional tale were retained, but sometimes there is so much variation that the description "fantasy on a theme" might be more appropriate. This license has long been understood to have been the minstrels' tradition, and secular music, including the repertory we are considering here, is clearly part of that tradition.

As noted above, the principles of instrumental and vocal ornamentation appear to be basically the same. Any difference between the two repertories lies in the quantity of ornaments used and the length of individual ornaments.[98] The smaller quantity found in vocal music was no doubt influenced in part by the requirements of textual clarity and consideration of the poetry; but the nature of the ornaments and their placement was the same in both. This is further evidence for the assumption that the two repertories, vocal and instrumental, were only different manifestations of a single performance aesthetic, and that the better-documented (or at least differently documented) minstrel tradition can be accepted as a basis for the performance of the instrumental repertory. The minstrels of the late Middle Ages did not divide

clearly into separate groups of singers and instrumentalists; a single enter-
tainer or group of entertainers frequently performed both functions.[99]

Ornamented Manuscripts

Evidence of the tradition of elaboration as it was applied to instrumental
performance is found in two manuscripts that contain instrumental elaborations of vocal compositions. It is particularly relevant to this discussion that
both manuscripts are also sources of dance compositions included here:
Nos.42–44 come from the Robertsbridge Codex, and Nos.45–47 from the
Faenza Codex. These two sources provide examples of late fourteenth- and
early fifteenth-century instrumental elaboration in English, Italian, and
French styles, thereby covering all the national styles included in the present
edition with the exception of the Czech ("Czaldy Waldy," No.30).[100]

In discussing the use of ornaments it is convenient to employ the late-
Renaissance distinction that ornaments *to* a particular note are called "graces"
and ornaments *between* notes are called "passaggi."[101] In actual practice one
type often flows directly into the next without a break, but the academic
distinction makes discussion easier. Most of Jerome's ornaments discussed
above can be considered "graces." The type of "reverberation" in which longer
notes are subdivided would be "passaggi."

"Graces" are not found written into the music of the medieval period, perhaps because they are so difficult to notate accurately.[102] Nor are they indicated
by sign, as they are in later centuries. Their detailed description in Jerome's
treatise is the only firm evidence that they were used. In modern terms, his
"graces" are known as vibrato, mordent, appoggiatura, and trills of various
kinds. The earliest surviving practical source that includes an indication of
graces, the mid-fifteenth-century Buxheimer MS,[103] contains only one sign
and is therefore of limited help in supporting Jerome's points.

The "grace" in the Buxheimer MS is written as a looped downward stem:
♩. It is found on notes with the value, ♪, ♩, and 𝅗𝅥; it always occurs on the beat;
it is often followed by the next highest scale note; and it is frequently followed
by a turn figure (see Example 2).

Although in modern transcriptions this ornament symbol is always marked
as a trill, there is no reason to support such a limited interpretation. The same
symbol stands for "mordent" in the 1520 *Fundamentum* of Johannes Buch-
ner,[104] but from Jerome's statements about appropriateness of placement, we
may conclude that it simply meant to apply a "grace," the specific figure to
be determined by the performer according to circumstances, as per the summary above. If interpreted in this way, the "grace" symbol in Buxheimer
reinforces Jerome's statements and can be considered a practical application
of some of his directions for ornament placement. We may conclude, therefore, that as early as the late thirteenth century, "graces" were added according
to the principles found in Jerome's treatise but without a specific sign in the
notation.

Ornaments of the "passaggi" type are found in the instrumental elaborations
of the Faenza and Robertsbridge codices. They can be as short as a few notes
(Example 3a) or quite long (Example 3b).

Example 2. From Buxheimer MS. a. "Annabasanna," fol. 51v. b. "Se le fatze
ay pale," fol. 47r. c. "Longus tenor," fol. 27v.

A comparison of the ornamented versions and the vocal originals of all the
compositions in the two manuscripts yields the following general principles
for the application of "passaggi"[105] (they cannot be applied to the repertory,
however, without the further consideration of style, see below):

1. The basic outline of the composition is usually retained. No ornaments
are placed in such a way as to obscure cadences or phrase endings. This is
accomplished by using longer rhythmic values at beginnings and ends of
phrases, a technique that tends to delineate the structure.

2. In a polyphonic composition most of the ornamentation is applied to
the upper part. The lower part receives only occasional rhythmic variation
and melodic subdivision.

3. The ornaments usually flow for several beats at a time.

4. The pitches of the original melody are usually incorporated into the
ornamental pattern, although exceptions can be found in the more-extended
passages.

5. The ornament passages can either retain the basic melodic shape of the
original or stray from it. Evidence of both is found.

6. Most ornaments are stepwise.

7. Rhythmic variation is also used, such as the substitution of triple rhythm
for duple or the reverse (see Example 4).

Example 3. From Faenza Codex. a. "Jour a jour la vie." b. "Non al suo amante."

8. The ornament passages mix both steady rhythmic patterns and long-short patterns, as in Example 4.

Additional ornament ideas can be found in the dances within this volume. Note the various quick-moving passages that can be considered

Robertsbridge (treble)

Vocal Original

Example 4. "Tribum quem," from Robertsbridge Codex.

ornament figures that would also have been improvised in place of the slower-moving notes.

Improvisation over a Cantus Firmus

The Faenza Codex also contains several treble improvisations over sacred *cantus firmi* from which one can extract principles applicable to the dance tenors included here:[106]

1. The added part is always above the tenor.
2. Perfect intervals are used at the beginnings and ends of phrases.
3. At the beginnings of mensural perfections perfect intervals are usually used, but examples of thirds and sixths can also be found.
4. The first note of each beat is usually consonant with the *cantus firmus*, but seconds, sevenths, and ninths are found in rapid-moving passages, as in Example 5, bar 4. As can be seen in Example 5, the dissonances usually occur on a beat other than the beginning of a mensural unit (bar, in the Faenza Codex).
5. Improvised lines contain a majority of stepwise passages.
6. The improvisor is free to use steady-flowing rhythms or to mix steady and irregular figures.
7. In addition to cadences over the final note of the *cantus firmus*, the improvisor is apparently free to choose secondary cadences. The notes selected were usually the modal final or dominant, but internal cadences on other notes can be found. The improvisor creates these cadences by forming a perfect interval over the *cantus firmus* and temporarily stopping the rhythmic motion. As can be seen in Example 5, the cadence is usually approached in contrary motion.

Although all the known *cantus firmi* in Faenza are sacred, exactly the same principles exist in the composition of dances Nos.45–47 from that source. It is probable, therefore, that tenors Nos.35–38 can be elaborated in this manner in the Italian style.

There are no additional obligations for the improvisor, who is free within

Example 5. Kyrie "Cunctipotens Genitor Deus," from Faenza Codex.

the bounds stated above (and those of the national musical style) to exercise personal creativity. It is recommended that anyone wishing to learn this technique should study the examples in the Faenza Codex. A feeling for national stylistic tendencies can be gained by observing the melodic and rhythmic patterns commonly found in the instrumental and vocal music of the late Middle Ages.

Improvising Additional Dance Material

Following the ideas of Wulf Arlt discussed above, modern performers should be able to continue to elaborate the existing compositions and invent some of their own in the styles of the Middle Ages. The basic compositional idea in all the dances is the use of a common refrain following a constantly changing verse. Arlt points out that in dance No.2, the refrain can consist of most of the material, with a verse of only a few notes. This would perhaps be the best place to begin since it requires the least amount of new material on the part of the fledgling improvisor. Simply add new notes preceding verse 1 in the style of the additions in verses 2 and 3. The added material should have melodic and rhythmic patterns similar to those already employed in the composition. The same technique can be applied to the French estampies, Nos.4–10, by adding new verses before the endings, using the melodic and rhythmic style of the already existing verses. Once this technique is mastered the creative performer may attempt the improvisation of an entire dance, inventing both verse and refrain in the style of those already existing.

For the dances from MS 29987 (Nos.14–28), which suggest eastern Mediterranean influence, a somewhat different approach can be taken. As the brief sample analysis of "Ghaetta" has shown, these works can be seen as elaborations of the individual notes of tetrachords. For improvisation and ornamentation in that style, the performer must first determine the tetrachords of the individual sections of any one composition, then proceed to elaborate the individual notes. Elaboration of any one note can take the form of rhythmic variations (as in Example 6a) or of short melodic patterns that continually return to the basic note (as in Example 6b). Study of those dances will provide a wide repertory of possible melodic and rhythmic patterns. A modern performer can simply supply a personal set of elaborations in place of those existing in a particular dance section, or invent an entire new section (or a complete dance). When inventing complete sections the performer must remember to place some emphasis on the modal final and dominant by elaboration of those notes in important structural positions, such as the opening, closing, and cadences. The separate *partes* of these dances sometimes have contrasting tetrachords, occasionally including chromatic variants of the initial tetrachords, but they return to the original tetrachords in the refrain.[107]

Example 6. From British Library, Additional 29987. a. "Isabella," opening section. b. "In Pro," *prima pars.*

PRELUDES AND POSTLUDES

Preludes and postludes are important parts of the performance of the dances. They are common in the folk music of Europe and the eastern Mediterranean, and were apparently a constant element in the performance of

both vocal and instrumental music of the Middle Ages.[108] Thomas Binkley
has explored the various types of preludes and postludes and has provided
examples that show how they may be constructed.[109] The purpose of a prelude
is to set the mode of the composition; therefore it must emphasize the modal
final and dominant and any other centers used in the piece to follow. Preludes
can be short or long, rhythmically free-flowing or regular, technically showy
or rather simple. They can contain important melodic or rhythmic motives
from the composition, but this is not necessary; an independent melodic-
rhythmic elaboration of the scale is also appropriate.

The presence of a postlude in both vocal and instrumental music is mentioned by Grocheio in his description of the *neupma*, or coda, added at the
end of an antiphon. He likens it to "an ending [that] may be played on the
vielle after a cantus coronatus or an estampie."[110] Constructed in a manner
similar to that of the prelude, the postlude rounds out the composition, extending the final cadence by emphasizing the scale and important notes of
the mode, especially the modal final.

DRONES

Drones had a prominent place in medieval performance; indeed some instruments could not play without a drone: bagpipe, hurdy-gurdy (and or-
ganistrum), and bowed strings with flat bridges. The close spacing of the
strings on plucked instruments (lute, gittern, etc.) along with the known tun-
ings suggest that those instruments, too, often played drone along with melody.[111] Drones can be added by the instrumentalist playing the melody or by
another performer. The drone note in most cases should be the modal final
or the dominant. In compositions that have extended sections revolving
around a tetrachord or a note outside the principal mode, the note repre-
senting the temporary tonal center may be chosen.

MONOPHONIC AND POLYPHONIC
PERFORMANCE

Performance procedure for a solo performer, or in the case of the polyphonic compositions, one to a part, is mostly self-evident. In addition to the
melody, solo performers would have added preludes, postludes, ornaments,
and drones as their creative contribution to the performance. For a monophonic composition with more than one performer, in the absence of medieval
documents explaining the practices, we must turn to folk music and music of
the eastern Mediterranean for possible clues.[112] The instruments in use by
these groups are very close to those of the Middle Ages, and the techniques
and practices employed agree with the small number of medieval discussions
of performance practice, which come not only from European sources but
also from Islam.[113] The following practices have been synthesized from those
traditions:

With more than one player, two basic procedures are possible and are found: sequential and simultaneous performance. In the first, individual instrumentalists take turns performing the melodies of the verses while the other members of the ensemble either rest or provide accompaniment. In the second, each performer ornaments the composition independently of the other(s). This results in occasional dissonances and sections with varied rhythms, but no attempt is made to eliminate them or to strive for identical ornamentation or variation. Both sequential and simultaneous performance are often present in the same composition, for example, when verses are performed by a soloist and the refrains are rendered by the ensemble.

These traditions and techniques deal only with monophonic music. The performance of polyphony was a European development, although the practices were undoubtedly closely connected to those for the performance of monophony. Many of the above performance suggestions can be adopted for the polyphonic dances, but with the following adjustments: doubling the lines is not recommended for the polyphonic dances; it would appear that polyphony was usually performed one to a part. And drones may not be appropriate in all polyphonic compositions because they tend to interfere with or negate the harmonic texture of the composition.[114] The suggestions for preludes, postludes, and ornaments, however, would all apply to polyphonic music.

Since the early 1960s, a growing number of early music ensembles have adopted the performance practices and techniques described here. The results are not only historically correct according to the evidence, but also, in the opinion of this writer, aesthetically pleasing and convincing in terms of what the music itself seems to be telling us. For the application of folk and Eastern traditions, there is less clear and direct evidence; but those practices provide the basis for a creative presentation of early music that, removed from any consideration of authenticity, is clearly vibrant and musical.

Notes

1. Curt Sachs. *World History of the Dance* (New York: W. W. Norton, 1937).

2. Ibid., pp.248–49.

3. On the use of dances in church, see Yvonne Rokseth, "Danses Cléricales du XIIIe siècle," in *Mélanges 1945 des Publications de la Faculté des Lettres de Strasbourg* (Paris, 1947), pp. 93–126; and Hans Spanke, "Tanzmusik in der Kirche des Mittelalters," *Neuphilologische Mitteilungen* 31 (1930):143–70.

4. A sixteenth-century account is included in Thoinot Arbeau, *Orchésographie*, 1596 (reprint Geneva: Minkoff, 1972), English translation by Mary Stewart Evans, *Orchesography* (reprint New York: Dover, 1967), p.13. In conversation, Thomas Binkley has related having witnessed dancing in churches in the Basque region in recent years.

5. "A ongni sera le fa raggunare il Signore colle trombette e arpe e liuti e insino a due ore si stormenta a danza," (letter from an unknown person in Pistoia to Piero di Basino de' Medici in Florence, dated 14 May 1439. Florence, Archivio di Stato, Mediceo Avanti il Principato, Filza II, No.512). My translation.

6. "Li rois, qui tant fu bials et gens, Molt dielement les conrea. Apriés mangier les envïa, tous ensamble de caroler" (Gerbert de Montreuil, "Le Roman de la violette", from *Le Roman de la Violette ou de Gerart de Nevers*, edited by Douglas L. Buffam [Paris: H. Champion, 1928], lines 90–94).

7. Geoffrey Chaucer's translation of *Le Roman de la Rose*, printed with French original in Ronald Sutherland, ed., *The Romaunt of the Rose and Le Roman de la Rose* (Berkeley and Los Angeles: University of California Press, 1968), lines 800–805.

8. "Li auquant chantent pastourelles; Le autre dïent en vielles, Chançons royaus et estempies, Danses, noctes et baleriez, En leüst, en psalterion, Chascun selonc s'entencion, Lais d'amours, descors et balades, Pour esbatre ces genz malades" (Jehan Maillart. *Le Roman du Comte d'Anjou*, edited by Mario Roques [Paris: H. Champion, 1931], lines 11–18). Translation by Marcia Epstein.

9. "E levate le tavole, con ciò fosse cosa che tutte le donne carolar sapessero, e similmente i giovani, e parte di loro ottimamente e sonare e cantare, comandò la reina che gli strumenti venissero; e per comandamento di lei Dioneo preso un liuto e la Fiammetta un viuola, cominciarono soavemente una danza a sonare. Per che la reina con l'altre donne, insieme co' due giovani presa una carola, con lento passo, mandati i famigliari a mangiare, a carolar cominciaron" (Giovanni Boccaccio, *Decameron*, edited by Cesare Segre [Milan: Mursia, 1966], Introduction to day 1, p.44). My translation.

10. These and other documents, such as pay records, are the sources of information found in modern scholarly studies of musicians and entertainers, for example, *Records of Early English Drama* (Toronto: University of Toronto Press, 1978–); and Constance Bullock-Davies, *Menestrellorum Multitudo: Minstrels at a Royal Feast* (Cardiff: University of Wales, 1978).

11. The only study known to me is Gabriele Christiane Busch, *Ikonographische Studien zum Solotanz im Mittelalter*, Innsbrucker Beiträge zur Musikwissenschaft, vol. 7, edited by W. Salmen (Innsbruck: Musikverlag Helbling, 1982). *Répertoire international d'iconographie musicale*, the *RIdIM Newsletter*, and the annual *Imago Musicae* are devoted to musical iconography. Art including dancing can be found among the representations in numerous studies of medieval social and art history, but the following studies especially involve investigation of musical images including dances: Howard M. Brown, "Trecento Angels and the Instruments They Play," in *Modern Musical Scholarship*, edited by Edward Olleson (Stockfield: Oriel Press, 1978), pp.112–40; Brown, "Fantasia on a

Theme by Boccaccio," *Early Music* 5 (1977):324–39; and Edmund A. Bowles, *La Pratique Musicale au Moyen Age / Musical Performance in the Late Middle Ages* (n.p.: Minkoff & Latte, 1983).

12. Additional material can be found in the sources quoted above and in Nigel Wilkins, *Music in the Age of Chaucer* (Cambridge: D. S. Brewer, 1979); Brown, "Fantasia on a Theme by Boccaccio"; Christopher Page, *Voices and Instruments of the Middle Ages: Instrumental practice and Songs in France 1100–1300* (London: J. M. Dent, 1987); John Stevens, *Words and Music in the Middle Ages: Song, Narrative, Dance and Drama, 1050–1350* (London: Cambridge University Press, 1986), chaps. 5 and 6.

13. Daniel Leech-Wilkinson points out the unsuspected riches to be found through this approach in his review of Christopher Page, *Voices and Instruments of the Middle Ages*. As Leech-Wilkinson expresses the issue: "To date, musicologists have been content to fish in the ocean of medieval writing with the coarsest of nets, pulling up the odd reference here and there to be stuffed and exhibited as evidence for broad generalizations about the practice of music" (*Journal of the Royal Musical Association* 113 [1988]:129). His point is as true for dance.

14. Among the scholars who have debated this point are Alfred Jeanroy, *Les Origines de la poésie français lyrique en France*, 3d ed. (Paris: H. Champion, 1925); Friedrich Gennrich, *Grundriss einer Formenlehre des mittelalterlichen Liedes* (Halle: Niemeyer, 1932); and Hans Spanke, *Beziehungen zwischen romanischen und mittellateinischen Lyrik* (Berlin, 1936). Their arguments are summarized in Gilbert Reaney, "Concerning the Origins of the Rondeau, Virelai and Ballade Forms," *Musica Disciplina* 6 (1952):155–66.

15. Margit Sahlin, *Étude sur la carole médiévale* (Uppsala: Almquist & Wiksells, 1940), concludes that the word "carol" derives originally from "Kyrie eleison" and in the Middle Ages (no date specified) came to mean dance song. Robert Mullally, "Cancon de carole," *Acta Musicologica* 58 (1986):224–31, relates the carol to a rondeau or rondeau-derived form.

16. Florence, Biblioteca Mediceo-Laurenziana, Pluteo 29.1. Facsimile, edited by Luther Dittmer, 2 vols., Publications of Mediaeval Musical Manuscripts 10 (Brooklyn: Institute of Mediaeval Music, n.d.).

17. Rokseth, "Danses cléricales." Transcriptions according to rhythmic modal ideas found in Rokseth and in Gordon A. Anderson, ed., *Notre Dame and Related Conductus, Opera Omnia*, vol. 8 (Henryville, Pa.: Institute of Mediaeval Music, n.d.).

18. Ernst Rohloff, *Die quellenhandschriften zum Musiktraktat des Johannes de Grocheio* (Leipzig: Deutscher Verlag, 1972).

19. "Nos autem solum illam rotundam vel rotundellum dicimus, cuius partes non habent diversum cantum a cantu responsorii vel refractus" (ibid., p.132).

20. See discussion of estampie and ductia below and the elaboration of this argument in Timothy J. McGee, "Medieval Dances: Matching the Repertory with Grocheio's Descriptions," *The Journal of Musicology* 7 (1989):498–517.

21. See, for example, Friedrich Gennrich, *Grundriss einer Formenlehre*; Jacques Handschin, "Über Estampie und Sequenz I and II," *Zeitschrift für Musikwissenschaft* 12 (1929):1–20 and 13 (1930):13–132; Lloyd Hibberd, "Estampie and Stantipes," *Speculum* 19 (1944):222–49; Helene Wagenaar-Nolthenius, "Estampie/Stantipes/Stampita," in *L'Ars Nova Italiana del Trecento* (Certaldo: n.p., 1968), pp.399–409; Patricia W. Cummins, "Le problème de la musique et de la poésie dans l'estampie," *Romania* 103 (1982):259–77; Kees Vellekoop, "Die Estampie: Ihre Besetzung und Funktion," *Basler Jahrbuch für historische Musikpraxis* 8 (1984):51–65.

22. Hibberd, "Estampie and Stantipes," p.232, equates "estampie," "stantipes," and "istanpitta."

23. "Partes autem ductiae et stantipedis puncta communiter dicuntur. Punctus autem est ordinata aggregatio concordantiarum harmoniam facientium ascendendo et descendendo, duas habens partes in principio similes, in fine differentes, quae clausum et apertum communiter appellantur" (Rohloff, p.136). All translations of Grocheio are mine, based on Albert Seay, *Johannes De Grocheo Concerning Music* (Colorado Springs: Colorado College of Music Press, 1973), p.20.

24. "Stantipes vero est sonus illitteratus, habens difficilem concordantiarum discretionem, per puncta determinatus. . . . Propter enim eius difficultatem facit animum

facientis circa eam stare et etiam animum advertentis. . . . Dico etiam per puncta determinatus, eo quod percussione, quae est in ductia, caret et solum punctorum distinctione cognoscitur" (Rohloff, p.136; Seay, p.20).

25. For a more detailed argument, see McGee, "Medieval Dances."

26. See Timothy J. McGee, "Eastern Influences in Medieval European Dances," in *Cross-Cultural Perspectives on Music*, edited by Robert Falck and Timothy Rice (Toronto: University of Toronto Press, 1982), pp.79–100.

27. See McGee, "Eastern Influences" and similar conclusions and speculations in Kenneth Zuckerman, "Improvisation in der mittelalterlichen Musik—eine Suche nach Lernmodellen," *Basler Jahrbuch für historische Musikpraxis* VII (1983):65–83. See also Ewald Jammers, "Studien zur Tanzmusik des Mittelalters," *Archiv für Musikwissenschaft* 30 (1973):81–95, which reduces the estampies in Bl 29987 to basic tone outlines. Lawrence Gushee, "Analytical Method and Compositional Process in Some Thirteenth- and Fourteenth-century Music," *Forum Musicologicum* 3 (1982):165–92, criticizes and expands on Jammers's approach.

28. Gilbert Reaney has also noticed that they may be dances. He found that the composition marked "Sangilio" and the one that follows it in the edition by Plamenac belong together as a single composition, excluding the fifteen measures mistakenly copied out of place from a composition that appears earlier in the manuscript; G. Reaney, review in *Journal of the American Musicological Society* 29 (1976):141, of Dragan Plamenac, *Keyboard Music of the Late Middle Ages in Codex Faenza 117* (Rome: American Institute of Musicology, 1972). It is interesting to note that these two compositions have some melodic characteristics in common with the elaborate estampies found in manuscript BL 29987 (Nos.14–21). The significance of this similarity is not currently understood.

29. See Camille Chabaneau, *Les biographies des troubadours in langue provençale* (Toulouse: Privat., 1885), pp.87–88. "Souvent souspire" is closely related to "Kalenda Maya," although there is little argrement among scholars as to which is the original and which the *contrafacta*. On this topic see Heinrich Husmann, "Kalenda maya," *Archiv für Musikwissenschaft* 10 (1953):275–79; Hendrik van der Werf, "Estampie," *The New Grove*, vol. 6, pp.254–58; and Gwynn S. McPeek, "Kalenda Maia: A Study in Form," *Medieval Studies in Honor of Robert White Linker* (n.p.: Editorial Castalia, 1973), pp.141–54.

30. Anonymous, *Doctrina de compondre dictatz*, ca. 1300; and Guillaume Molinier, *Leys d'amors*, early fourteenth century. Quoted and translated in Hibberd, "Estampie and Stantipes," p.224.

31. See discussion in McGee, "Medieval Dances."

32. "Est autem ductia sonus illitteratus, cum decenti percussione mensuratus. Dico autem illitteratus, quia, licet in voce humana fieri possit et per figuras repraesentari, non tamen per litteras scribi potest, quia littera et dictamine caret. Sed cum recta percussione, eo quod ictus eam mensurant et motum facientis et excitant animum hominis ad ornate movendum secundum artem, quam ballare vocant, et eius motum mensurant in ductiis et choreis" (Rohloff, p.136; Seay, p.20).

33. Siegmund Levarie, "Communications," *Journal of the American Musicological Society* 27 (1974):367–69.

34. "Sed si haec omnia subtiliter considerentur, inveniuntur a percussione fieri, cum omnis sonus percutiendo causetur, prout in sermonibus de anima comprobatum est" (Rohloff, p.133; Seay, p.19).

35. Stevens, *Words and Music*, pp.163–71; Page, *Voices and Instruments*, pp.77–84.

36. Page, *Voices and Instruments*, pp.81–83; McGee, "Medieval Dances."

37. This is the reasoning behind the translation of the Grocheio passage above, concerning the nature of the ductia, in which I have translated "ductia" as line dance in order to distinguish it from "choreis," round dance.

38. See McGee, "Medieval Dances."

39. No.11 does not have indications that the versicles should be repeated, but Grocheio states that double versicles are a feature of all secular dances, and thus a division into open and close endings has been proposed in the edition.

40. "Sunt tamen aliquae notae vocatae quattuor punctorum, quae ad ductiam vel stantipendem imperfectam reduci possunt" (Rohloff, p.136; Seay, p.20).

41. Quoted in Willi Apel, *Gregorian Chant* (Bloomington and London: Indiana University Press, 1958), p.175. I am indebted to David McCartney for bringing this to my attention.

42. Both compositions are transcribed and discussed in Gennrich, *Grundriss einer Formenlehre*, pp.167–74; "La Note Martinet" is transcribed in Handschin, "Über Estampie," pp.127–28. Also see Gustave Reese, *Music in the Middle Ages* (New York: W. W. Norton, 1940), pp.226–27; and Andrew Hughes, "The *Ludus super Anticlaudianum* of Adam de la Bassée," *Journal of the American Musicological Society* XXIII (1970):1–25. See detailed discussion in McGee, "Medieval Dances."

43. See Handschin, "Über Estampie," p.8. Another interpretation of the composition is that it consists of "model phrases" for didactic purposes; see Wulf Arlt, "The 'Reconstruction' of Instrumental Music: the Interpretation of the Earliest Practical Sources," in *Studies in the Performance of Late Medieval Music*, edited by Stanley Boorman (Cambridge: Cambridge University Press), pp.75–100; and Arlt, "Instrumentalmusik im Mittelalter: Fragen der Rekonstruktion einer schriftlosen Praxis," *Basler Jahrbuch für historische Musikpraxis* 7 (1983):48–54.

44. See facsimile in Harry E. Wooldridge, *Early English Harmony* (London: Stainer and Bell, 1897), vol. 1, Plate 24; John Stainer, *Early Bodleian Music* (reprint, Farnborough: Gregg, 1967), vol. 1, Plate 7; and Wulf Arlt, "Instrumentalmusik im Mittelalter," p.51.

45. See Meredith Ellis Little, "Saltarello," *The New Grove*, vol. 16, pp.430–32, and the discussion of the ballo, below.

46. Nos.27 and 28 are also melodically similar to each other.

47. "Amoroso in doi," in MS Paris, BN, f. ital. 476, f. 58v; "Amoroso, tre ballano," in Siena, Bibl. Com. L V 29, f. 71r; "Amoroso isghuardo in dua," in New York, Public Library *MGZMB-Res. 72–254, f. 27v. Music in MS 476, f. 63v; transcribed in Otto Kinkeldey, "Dance Tunes of the Fifteenth Century," in *Instrumental Music*, edited by David G. Hughes (Cambridge: Harvard University Press; reprint New York: Da Capo, 1972), pp.89–90.

48. Sachs, *World History*, p.294, suggests derivation from "rompere," to break, but the correct spelling for "broken" is "rotto."

49. For a different opinion, see ibid., pp.294–95.

50. For the most recent summaries of information on the subject see, "Dance," in *The New Grove*, vol. 5, pp.180–86; and Meredith Little, "Recent research in European dance, 1400–1800," *Early Music* 14 (1986):4–14.

51. Domenico da Piacenza, *De arte saltandi et choreas ducendii*, Paris, Bibl. Nat. fonds ital. 972.

52. See Ingrid Brainard, "Bassedanse, Bassadanza and Ballo in the 15th Century," in *Dance History Research: Perspectives from Related Arts and Disciplines*, edited by Joann W. Kealiinohomoku (n.p., 1970), pp.64–79; Brainard, *The Art of Courtly Dancing in the Early Renaissance* (West Newton, Mass.: n.p., 1981); Giulio Cattin, "Canti, canzoni a ballo e danze nelle Maccheronee di teofilo Folengo," *Revista Italiana di Musicologia* X (1975):180–215; Federico A. Gallo, "Il 'Ballare Lombardo' Circa 1435–1475," *Studi Musicali* VIII (1979):61–84; W. Thomas Marrocco, "Fifteenth-Century Ballo and Bassadanza: a Survey," *Studi Musicali* X (1981):31–41; Marrocco, *Inventory of 15th Century Bassedanze, Balli and Balletti* (n.p., Cord, 1981); Marrocco, "The Derivation of Another Bassadanza," *Acta Musicologica* 51 (1979):137–39; and Barbara Sparti, "The 15th-Century *balli* tunes: a new look," *Early Music* 14 (1986):346–57.

53. Described in Brainard, "Bassedanse, Bassadanza"; and Sparti, "15th-century *Balli* tunes."

54. Listed in Brainard, *The Art of Courtly Dancing*, pp.6–8; Gallo, "Il 'Ballare Lombardo'"; and Marrocco, *Inventory*.

55. Cattin, "Canti," p.70. The evidence includes two other *ballo* names that appear to be related to Ferrara: "Belriguardo," the name of the palace constructed for Nicolò III in 1435; and "Leoncello," possibly referring to Leonello d'Este, son of Nicolò III. The author of the earliest dance manual in which the ballo "Belfiore" appears, Dominico da Piacenza, is known to have worked at Ferrara in the early decades of the fifteenth century. On the possible association of the Faenza Codex with Ferrara, see

Adriano Cavicchi, "Sacro e profano. Documenti e note su Bartolomeo da Bologna e gli organisti della cattedrale di Ferrara nel primo Quattrocento," *Revue Italiana di Musicologia* X (1975):46–71; and Timothy J. McGee, "Instruments and the Faenza Codex," *Early Music* 14 (1986):480–90.

56. See Otto Kinkeldey, "Dance Tunes of the Fifteenth Century," in *Instrumental Music*, edited by David G. Hughes. (Cambridge: Harvard University Press, 1959; reprint, New York: Da Capo Press, 1972), pp.89–152.

57. In MS Perugia, Bibl. Communale 431, fol. 105v–106. See discussion and transcription in Manfred Bukofzer, *Studies in Medieval and Renaissance Music* (New York: W. W. Norton, 1950), pp.190–216.

58. See Sparti, "15th-century *Balli* tunes," p.354.

59. See Lewis Lockwood, *Music in Renaissance Ferrara, 1400–1505* (Cambridge: Harvard University Press, 1984), chap. 10; Reinard Strom, in his review of Lockwood (*Music and Letters*, 1986, pp.284–85), suggests that the famous Ferrara lutenist Pietrobono de Burzelis may have been from Brussels and his teacher Leonardo from Germany. See also Keith Polk, "Civic Patronage and Instrumental Ensembles in Renaissance Florence," *Augsburger Jahrbuch für Musikwissenschaft* III (1986):51–67.

60. See Timothy J. McGee, *Medieval and Renaissance Music: A Performer's Guide* (Toronto: University of Toronto Press, 1985), pp.190–200; Keith Polk, "The Foundations of Ensemble Improvisation in the Late Fifteenth Century," unpublished article; Timothy Aarset, "Basse Danse Improvisation ca. 1500," *Proceedings of the Dance History Scholars Conference*, 1982; and Aarset, "Toward a Definition of Polyphonic Ensemble Improvisation circa 1500," *Fifteenth-Century Studies* 4 (1980):1–16. Also see "Performance Practices," below.

61. They are called "the oldest Czech dance compositions" by Václav Plocek, "K problematice nasich nejstarsich tanecnich skladeb," *Hudebni Veda* 6 (1969):3–25; and again in Plocek, "Jeste k problematice Czaldy waldy," *Hudebni Veda* 7 (1970):46–57; and in Plocek, "Zur Problematik der ältesten tschechischen Tanzkompositionen," *Studia Musicologica* 13 (1971):241–47; but the author never adequately discusses the reason for identifying the music with dance.

62. Rohloff, p.136. On the strength of this reference they were identified as dances by Pierre Aubry, *Recherches sur les "Tenors" français dans les motets du treizeime siècle* (Paris: H. Champion, 1907), pp.32–34.

63. Montpellier, Bibl. de la Faculté de Médecine, H 196.

64. I have excluded from the count the two texted dances Nos.1a and 1b, and the fragment No.42.

65. See Arlt, "The 'Reconstruction'."

66. See McGee, "Eastern Influences."

67. "A tant ont lez napes leveez, Et quant orent lez mains laveez, Sont les querolez commenchiez. Cez dames qui ont voiz seriez A chanter prennent haultement; Chascun lez respont lïement, Qui bien sot chanter si chanta:" (Jehan Maillart, *Le Roman du Comte d'Anjou*, lines 2875–81).

68. Rohloff, p.132; Seay, p.17.

69. Geoffrey Chaucer, *The Romaunt of the Rose*, lines 759–62.

70. Ibid., lines 779–88.

71. "Tel carole ne fu pas veue Pres d'une quart dure d'une lieue" (Phelipe de Remi, from "La Manekine," cited in Sachs, *World History*, p.271).

72. Chaucer, from "The Knight's Tale," cited in Wilkins, *Music in the Age of Chaucer*, p.102.

73. "Tres que n'avoie que .xii. ans, Estoie forment goulousans De veoir danses et caroles, D'oïr menestrels et paroles" (Jean Froissart, *L'espinette amoureuse*, edited by Anthime Fourrier [Paris: Klincksieck, 1963], lines 27–30). Translation from Wilkins, *Music in the Age of Chaucer*, p.2.

74. "Et si trestost que cesse eurent Les estampies qu'il batoient, Chil et chelles qui s'esbatoient Au danser, sans gaires atendre, Commenchierent leurs mains a tendre Pour caroler" (Froissart, *L'espinette*, lines 358–63). Translation from Wilkins, *Music in the Age of Chaucer*, p.2.

75. Moser, "Stantipes und Ductia," and Sachs, *World History*, both translate "stan-

tipes" in this way. Hibberd, "Estampie and Stantipes," p.223, associates it with the French and Provençal verb "estampir," to resound.

76. The bassadanza, balli, and basse danse sources are listed in Gallo, "Il 'Ballare Lombardo' "; Marrocco, *Inventory*; Brainard, *The Art of Courtly Dancing*, pp.5–8; and Frederick Crane, *Materials for the Study of the Fifteenth Century Basse Danse* (Brooklyn: Institute of Mediaeval Music), 1968.

77. "Dance," *The New Grove*, vol. 5, p.181.

78. Ibid., pp.183–84.

79. Ibid., p.180.

80. The case here is made for the Italian tradition because of the absence of material from the other countries, but it would appear that the changes in Italy were closely paralleled in France. See Brainard, "Bassedanse, Bassadanza."

81. "Dance," pp.183–84.

82. Jammers, "Studien zur Tanzmusik des Mittelalters." But see Lawrence Gushee's further reductions using the same technique and his reservations about the results of this type of analysis, in "Analytical Method and Compositional Process," pp.165–91.

83. Zuckermann, "Improvisation in der mittelalterlichen Musik"; and McGee, "Eastern Influences."

84. Handschin, "Über Estampie."

85. See Karl Signell, *Makam: Modal Practice in Turkish Art Music* (Providence: Asian Music Publications, 1977).

86. See Liberty Manik, *Das arabische Tonsystem im Mittelalter* (Leiden: E. J. Brill, 1969); and George Dimitri Sawa, "Music Performance Practice in the Early ʿAbbasid Era, 132 A.H./750 A.D.–320A.H./932 A.D.," Ph.D. diss., University of Toronto, 1983, chap. 2.

87. Wulf Arlt, "The 'reconstruction' "; followed up in Arlt, "Instrumentalmusik in Mittelalter," pp.32–64.

88. "Mais qui vei'st après mengier, Venir menestrels sans dangier, Pingniez et mis en puré corps! La firent mains divers acors. Car je vi la tout en un cerne, Viële, rubebe, guiterne. . . . Et certeinnement, il me semble, Qu'onques mais tele melodie, Ne fu veüe ne oïe, Car chascuns d'eaus, selonc l'acort, De son instrument, sans descort, Viële, guiterne, citole, harpe, trompe, corne, flajole, Pipe, souffle, muse, naquaire, Taboure, et quanque on puet faire, De dois, de penne et de l'archet, Oÿ j'et vi en ce parchet.

"Quant fait eurent une estampie, Les dames et leur compaignie, S'en alerent, ci deus, ci trois, En elles tenant par les dois, Jusqu'en une chambre moult belle;" (Guillaume de Machaut, "Remède de Fortune," in *Oeuvres*, edited by Ernest Hoeppfner, 3 vols. [Paris: Firmin-Didot, 1908–21], vol. II, lines 3957–62, 3976–91). Translation by Robert Taylor.

89. For commentary and listings of many of these sources see Vellekoop, "Die Estampie: Ihre Besetzung und Funktion," pp. 51–65. For a detailed discussion of instruments in the Middle Ages see Thomas Binkley, "Zur Aufführungspraxis der einstimmigen Musik des Mittelalters; ein Werkstattbericht," *Basler Jahrbuch für Historische Musikpraxis* I (1977):42–50.

90. "Bonus autem artifex in viella omnem cantum et cantilenam et omnem formam musicalem generaliter introducit" (Rohloff, p.136).

91. "Li servant adonc se hasterent, Erranment les napes osterent. .iiii. menestreil de vïele, Ont une estampie nouviele, Devant la dame vielee" (Jean de Condé, from "La Messe des Oisaus et li plais des chanonesses et des grises nonains," lines 639–43, in August Scheler, ed., *Dits et contes de Baudouin de Condé et de son fils Jean de Condé*, 3 vols. [Brussels: V. Devaux, 1866–67]).

92. For a quick guide to instruments in their appropriate time and location see McGee, *Medieval and Renaissance Music*, pp.63–75.

93. On tempo, see Willi Apel, *The Notation of Polyphonic Music 900–1600*, 5th ed. (Cambridge: The Mediaeval Academy of America, 1961); J. A. Bank, *Tactus, Tempo and Notation in Mensural Music from the 13th to the 17th Century* (Amsterdam: A. Bank, 1972); Salvatore Gullo, *Das Tempo in der Musik des XIII. und XIV. Jahrhunderts* (Bern: P. Haupt, 1964); Curt Sachs, *Rhythm and Tempo* (New York: W. W. Norton, 1953).

94. Heironymus de Moravia, O.P., *Tractatus de Musica*, edited by Simon M. Cserba, O. P. (Regensburg: Friedrich Pustet, 1935), chap. 25, pp.183–90. Translation of this section in Carol MacClintock, *Readings in the History of Music in Performance* (Bloomington: Indiana University Press, 1979), pp.3–7. See also similar comments at the end of Jerome's treatise, in which there are quotations from Johannes de Garlandia's *De mensurabili Musica*, translated by Stanley H. Birnbaum, in Johannes de Garlandia, *Concerning Measured Music*, Colorado College of Music Press Translations No.9 (Colorado Springs: Colorado College of Music Press, 1978), pp.51–55.

95. Given the wide use of vibrato in Eastern music and folk music of all kinds and its obvious availability as a way of embellishing a vocal tone, I am suggesting that here Jerome may be considering vocal vibrato and trill as the same ornament. His statement about certain types of the harmonic flower "not exceeding a semitone" (see below) reinforces this and suggests that he is accepting minute pitch variation—narrow vibrato—as a type of trill.

96. Examples of variant readings can be found in Hendrik van der Werf, *The Chansons of the Troubadours and Trouvères* (Utrecht: A. Oosthoek, 1972).

97. For a more detailed discussion of this point see Binkley, "Zur Aufführungspraxis," pp.38–42.

98. See McGee, *Medieval and Renaissance Music*, pp.157–60.

99. See Page, *Voices and Instruments*.

100. For a further discussion of styles see McGee, *Medieval and Renaissance Music*, chap 7; and McGee, "Ornamentation, National Styles, and the Faenza Codex," *Early Music New Zealand*, 1987, pp.3–14.

101. This practice is used in Howard Mayer Brown, *Embellishing 16th Century Music* (London: Oxford University Press, 1976), p.1.

102. It is thought by some that tiny circles above certain notes in the Robertsbridge-Codex may be symbols for graces. There is no evidence to support this theory.

103. Facsimile edition by Bertha Wallner (Kassel: Bärenreiter, 1955); modern transcription in *Das Erbe Deutscher Musik* vols. 37–39 (1935–).

104. Edition in C. Paesler, "Das Fundamentbuch von Hans von Constanz," *Vierteljahrsschrift für Musikwissenschaft* V (1889); discussion in Apel, *Notation*, p.24.

105. I acknowledge that I am choosing all my examples from instrumental elaborations of vocal music. There are no known examples of elaborations of "unadorned" instrumental works from the period, but the discussion in Jerome's treatise suggests, as I state above, that the difference between the two was in quantity rather than in type or placement.

106. For a more basic approach to the improvisation of two-part counterpoint see McGee, *Medieval and Renaissance Music*, pp.189–97.

107. I cannot explain the technique in use in Nos. 19 and 20, which have two different sets of refrains employing different tetrachords.

108. See Howard Ferguson, "Prelude," *The New Grove*, vol. 15, pp.210–12; and McGee, *Medieval and Renaissance Music*, pp.115–18.

109. Binkley, "Zur Aufführungspraxis," pp.53–64.

110. "Est autem neupma quasi cauda vel exitus sequens antiphonam, quemadmodum in viella post cantum coronatum vel stantipedem exitus" (Rohloff, p.255).

111. For more on the subject of drone instruments, see Timothy J. McGee, "The Social Status of Drone Instruments," *Continuo* 7 (1984):9–12.

112. An extended discussion of medieval performance practices in the light of eastern Mediterranean influence, including instrumental combinations and instrumental performance techniques, can be found in Binkley, "Zur Aufführungspraxis," pp.19–75.

113. The treatises of al-Farabi and al-Isbahani are discussed in detail in Sawa, "Music Performance Practice."

114. For further information on late medieval European instrumentation, see Howard Mayer Brown, "Instruments and Voices in the Fifteenth-Century Chanson," in *Current Thought in Musicology* (Austin and London: University of Texas Press, 1976), pp.89–137.

THE DANCES

Editorial Practices

In transcribing the music into modern notation I have attempted to retain as much of the original as possible, without cluttering the page or confusing the reader. Those wishing to compare the transcriptions with the original notation should consult the sources of the facsimiles given in the Critical Notes.

For those compositions whose original sources show no divisions into bars, a form of *mensurstrich*, rather than modern bar lines, has been adopted to indicate the regular mensural division. This system avoids the need to use modern tied notes. More importantly, it gives the reader a much clearer view of the flow and general contour of the melodic line, similar to that provided by the original notation. This form of marking should facilitate the visualization of the rhythmic flow into units both larger and smaller than the modern "bar." Bar lines found in the Faenza Codex (Nos.45–47) are reproduced in the transcription.

In the original manuscripts the endings, refrains, and sectional repeats are usually written only once and indicated thereafter by signs. For the reader's convenience I have written out these repeats but included them, as well as all other material not in the original, in square brackets.

Ligatures are not indicated in the transcriptions, but it can be seen from the incipits that they are present in most of the compositions. Since their use in this repertory would be solely to indicate rhythmic values unambiguously, they are superfluous in modern notation. Further, because in some of the dances ligatures are ubiquitous, I found the editorial bracket symbol obtrusive and confusing, and thus I have not included it.

One of the most controversial issues in the editing of medieval music involves accidentals: the use of b-flat, which was a legitimate member of the scale; the application of *musica ficta*; and especially the duration for which any noted accidental should be applied. An additional problem encountered in these manuscripts is that accidentals are often placed well before the notes to which they refer. In a few cases this has required editorial judgment as to exactly which note is to be changed. My choice here has been extremely conservative. No accidentals are applied that have not already appeared in the composition; and I do not raise the penultimate note to heighten a sense of cadence unless there is an analogous situation marked in the manuscript. But even within this general editorial policy there was still the problem of deciding how long an accidental should remain in effect. I have made my judgments according to the tonal orientation of the individual phrase, retaining an accidental until the tone center has changed. Editorial accidentals are placed above the notes. Redundant accidentals have been silently omitted.

Spellings within the compositions have been silently regularized—e.g., *chiusso/chiuso*; *sechunda/secunda*—but the titles have retained their manuscript spellings with the exception of "Dança Amorosa," which is spelled "Danança" in the source.

As stated on p. 27 above, I have included in the Critical Notes the transcription value I believe to be the counting unit for each dance; that is, the note value that should be considered when establishing the "heartbeat" speed. But the reader is warned that the counting unit is not necessarily the basic metric unit for the composition, any more than the *mensurstrich* is. The metric organization and melodic-rhythmic flow of the composition should be derived from the melody itself. For example, the counting unit of dance 1a, "Kalenda Maya," is the dotted half note, but the metric flow is actually 6/4, subdivided variously into two groups of three and three groups of two. Similarly, all the dances given in *trecento* notation have the *breve* as the unit of basic measure, but in the various dances the meter is sometimes subdivided into single units of 2/4 or 6/8, and at other times it flows over two or three bars.

1a. Kalenda Maya

Kalenda Maia

I

Neither May Day nor the beech tree's leaves nor the song of birds nor gladiolus flowers are pleasing to me, noble and vivacious lady, until I receive a swift messenger from your fair person to tell me of some new pleasure that love brings me; and may I be joined to you and drawn toward you, perfect lady; and may the jealous one fall stricken before I must leave you. [And may I be joined ...]

II

My sweet beloved, for the sake of God, may the jealous one never laugh at my pain, for his jealousy would be very costly if it were to separate two such lovers; for I would never be joyful again, nor would joy be of any benefit to me without you; I would set out on such a road that no one would ever see me again; on that day would I die, worthy lady, that I lost you. [And may I be joined...]

III

How shall my lady be lost, or restored to me, if she has not yet been mine? For a man or woman is not a lover just by thinking so. But when a suitor is accepted as a lover, the reputation that he gains is greatly enhanced, and the attractive appearance causes much stir; but I have not held you naked nor conquered you in any other sense; I have only desired you and believed in you, without any further encouragement. [And may I be joined...]

IV

I should not likely find pleasure if I should ever be separated from you, Fair Knight, in anger; for my being is not turned toward anyone else, my desire does not draw me to anyone else, for I desire none but you. I know that this would be pleasing to slanderers, my lady, since this is the only thing that would satisfy them. There are those who would be grateful to you if they were to see or feel my suffering, since they admire you and think presumptuously about that which makes the heart sigh. [And may I be joined...]

V

Lady Beatrice, your worth is so refined by its nature, and it develops and grows beyond that of all other ladies; in my opinion you enhance your dominance with your merit and your admirable speech without fail; you are responsible for initiating praiseworthy actions; you have wisdom patience and learning; incontestably, you adorn your worth with benevolence. [And may I be joined...]

VI

Worthy lady, everyone praises and proclaims your merit which is so pleasing; and whoever would forget you places little value on his life; therefore I worship you, distinguished lady, for I have singled you out as the most pleasing and the best, accomplished in worth, and I have courted you and served you better then Eric did Enide. Lord Engles* I have constructed and completed the estampida. [And may I be joined...]

* Boniface, Marquis of Monferrat, patron.

1b. Souvent Souspire

1. Sou- vent sou- spi- re   mon cuer plein d'i- re   pour la
2. Dex s'or po- voi- e   te- nir la voi- e   par quoi
3. Tant ai ser- vi- e   ma douce a- mi- e   bien croi
4. E- le se pai- ne   de me tre en pai- ne   moi tou-
5. De m' am- i- e   m'es- tuet re- tre- re   quant voil

1. plus be- le de l'en- pi- re.   Si me mar- ti- re   que ne l'os
2. g'e us- se de li joi- e.   as- sez au- roi- e   plus ne quer-
3. que q'en per- drai la vi- e.   Quant je la pri- e   el me dit
4. te lon- gue la se- mai- ne.   Si me de- mai- ne   com sien de-
5. que je ne li puis ple- re.   E- le est tant dou- ce   et de- bo-

1. di- re.   Sou- vent mi fet plo- rer et ri- re.   E- le mi
2. roi- e;   tant ne de- sir dras ne mou- noi- e.   Douz Dex s'a-
3. vi- e;   Fui de ci gars je ne t'aim mi- e.   Douz Dex s'a-
4. mai- ne;   plus est fie- re que chas- te- lai- ne.   On- ques ne
5. ne- re   qu'el ne por- roit a nul de- sple- re.   Dex por- quoi

1. set bien e- scon- di- re   et moi seur touz au- tres de- spi- re.
2. mor tant mi guer- roi- e!   Quant el ne veut que je sein soi- e
3. mor mi con- tra- li- e   qui en mon cuer s'est en- dor- mi- e.
4. fu si be- leE lai- ne   ne n'ot on- ques si douce a- lai- ne.
5. m'est el si con- tre- re   qu'el ne pri- se riens mon a- fe- re?

1 De- scri- re en ci- re   ne por- roit nus son cors ne li- re.
2. le foi- e mi noi- e   plus ai do- lor que cil de Troi- e.
3. N'est mi- e en vi- e   qui m' en poist don- ner a- i- e.
4. Es trai- ne de pai- ne   mi fet ne- is au di a e- mai- ne.
5. A- tre- re la he- re   m'e- stuet, quant je ne li puis ple- re.

1. O- ci- re de fri- re   mi fet quant la re- mi- re.
2. Ne croi- e que noi- e   le jor que sire en soi- e
3. M'a- mi- e ma vi- e de vous ai grant en vi- e
4. vi- lai- ne n'a vai- ne qui d'or gueil ne soit plai- ne.
5. re- tre- re me fe- re m'e- stuet de son re- pe- re.

De- scri- re en ci- re   ne por- roit nus son cors ne li- re.

O- ci- re de fri- re mi fet quant la re- mi- re.

52

I

Often my heart full of grief sighs for the most beautiful one in the empire. She torments me so much that I dare not describe it. Often she makes me weep and laugh. She knows well how to refuse me and to despise me more than all others. No one could describe her body on wax, nor read about it. When I look at her she kills me and sets me on fire. [No one could describe...]

II

God, if now I could be set on the path by which I would obtain joy from her I would have enough. I would not ask for anything more; I do not wish as strongly for clothing nor money. Sweet Lord, her love would cure me so completely! When she doesn't want me to be hers my liver fails me, I have more pain than the fellow from Troy. I do not believe that I will see the day when I will be master of her. [No one could describe...]

III

So long have I served my sweet beloved that I believe truly that it will cost me my life. When I entreat her she replies with refusal: 'Get out of here, fellow, I don't love you at all!' Sweet Lord, the love for her that has settled into my heart is fighting against me. There's no one alive who can give me help. My love, my life, I desire you greatly. [No one could describe...]

IV

She takes pains to hurt me all week long. She treats me like her domain; she is more haughty than a chatelaine. Never was there such a fair Helen, nor one with such sweet breath. She rewards me with pain even on Sunday. There is not a wench so weak that she is not full of spitefulness. [No one could describe...]

V

I must renounce my beloved since I see that I cannot please her. She is so sweet and seemly that she could not displease anyone. God, why is she so opposed to me that she takes no thought for my good: I must draw grief onto myself since I cannot please her. I must make myself leave her presence. [No one could describe...]

2.

3. [La Prime Estampie Royal]

✳ manuscript stops

4. La Seconde Estampie Royal

5. La Tierche Estampie Roial

6. La Quarte Estampie Royal

7. La Quinte Estampie Real

8. La Seste Estampie Real

9. La Septime Estampie Real

10. La Uitime Estampie Real

11. Dansse Real

12.

13. Danse

14. Ghaetta

73

15. Chominciamento di Gioia

Terza Pars

Quarta Pars

Quinta Pars

16. Isabella

79

Quarta Pars

17. Tre Fontane

Prima Pars

1. Aperto

84

Quarta Pars

18. Belicha

19. Parlamento

20. In Pro

1. Aperto

2. Chiuso

Quinta Pars

100

21. Principio di Virtu

22. Salterello [1]

Prima Pars

1. Aperto

2. Chiuso

Secunda Pars

1.

23. Salterello [2]

24. Salterello [3]

25. Salterello [4]

26. Lamento di Tristano

La Rotta

27. La Manfredina

La Rotta della Manfredina

28. Trotto

29. Dança Amorosa

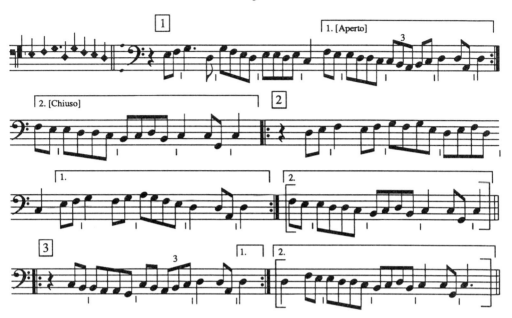

Troto

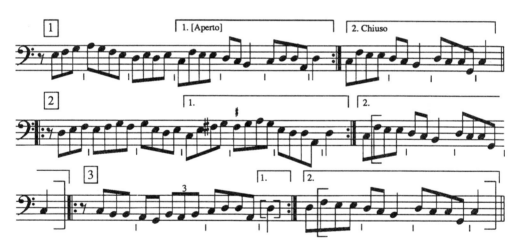

30. Czaldy Waldy

Czaldy Waldy

R[epetiti]o

31. Chose Tassin [1]

32. Chose Tassin [2]

33   Chose Tassin [3]

34. Chose Loyset

35. Chançoneta Tedescha [1]

Secunda Pars

36. Chançona Tedescha [2]

Secunda Pars

37 Chançona Tedescha [3]

38. Chançona Tedescha [4]

39.

CANTUS SUPERIOR

CANTUS INFERIOR

126

40.

CANTUS SUPERIOR

CANTUS INFERIOR

41.

CANTUS SUPERIOR

CANTUS INFERIOR

42.

43.

d g s g s f ♮

133

Tertius Punctus

Quartus Punctus

44. Petrone

Tercius Punctus

Quartus Punctus

Quintus Punctus

45. Tumpes

148

46. Sangilio

1. Aperto

2. [Chiuso]

47. Bel Fiore Dança

Secunda Pars

Critical Notes

With the exception of Nos. 1b and 30, the dances are all unica and are found in widely varied sources. The manuscripts are from the thirteenth, fourteenth, and early fifteenth centuries, and originate in England (3), France (10), Italy (3), and Czechoslovakia (2). They employ a variety of notations, including modal rhythm, French and Italian mensural notation, and keyboard tablature (a combination of notes and letters). The sources, their notations, and the editorial solutions are discussed below. The following abbreviations are used: n. = note; mx = maxima; l = longa; b = breve; sb = semibreve; m = minim; sm = semiminim. For complete citations of the facsimiles and transcriptions listed for individual dances, see pp. 175–77 below.

No. 1a. Kalenda Maya   vocal estampie

Counting unit: ♩
Unique music source: Paris, Bibliothèque Nationale, fonds français 22543, fol. 62r.
Sources of text:
Paris, B. N. fonds fr. 22543, fol. 62r, 519.
Paris, B. N. fonds fr. 856, fol. 125 (unique source of verse 5).
Paris, B. N. fonds fr. 12474, fol. 106.
Barcelona, Bibl. de Catalunya 146, fol. 59.

The author of the text of "Kalenda Maya" is troubadour Raimbaut de Vaqueiras (ca. 1155–1205), but the story that he wrote the poem to a melody he heard performed by two jongleurs at the court of Montferrat is questionable, see above, p. 10.

MS 22543, the only source of the music, was copied in western Provence ca. 1300. It is one of two surviving books devoted entirely to the transmission of troubadour songs with their melodies; it contains 950 poems, 160 with melodies.[1]

The most common system in use for the rhythmic interpretation of twelfth- and thirteenth-century monophonic music follows the theory developed at the turn of the present century by Jean Beck and Pierre Aubry: The shapes of the neumes are ignored, and long and short values are assigned according to the stresses in the syllables of the poetry.[2] This theory has been seriously questioned recently as being arbitrary and unfounded in either the theories of the Middle Ages or the notation.[3] There are no known treatises that deal with rhythm in monophonic music, and thus I have chosen to follow the only other available guide—the principles established in theoretical writings for the notation of polyphonic music. Throughout the manuscript neumes are used in patterns that suggest that their shapes are intentionally chosen and therefore may well signify duration, as they do in polyphony. The scribe of "Kalenda Maya" has used the longa as the basic neume with occasional ligatures and plicas. My transcription interprets each neume mensurally, resulting in a composition that is almost totally isosyllabic. The caesura mark is interpreted to be a phrase mark but without specific value; its value is adjusted to the needs of the text stresses. That is, the caesura marks at the end of the note for *faia* (bar 2) and *glaia* (bar 4) are similar, but the text stress requires different rest lengths. They only deviation from strict isosyllabic transcription is in the assignment of a half note instead of a quarter note to the last syllable in a full phrase. The neume ♩ has been interpreted as l, mx (♩♩) in line 5, n. 4, 5.

The repeat of the refrain is editorial,[4] and it is suggested that the last four lines of verse 1 be sung to this section following each stanza. Text edition from Joseph Linskill, *The Poems of the Troubadour Raimbaut de Vaqueiras* (The Hague: Mouton & Co., 1964), pp. 185–87. Translation by Robert Taylor.

Facsimile:
McPeek, "Medieval Monophonic Song," p.3.

Transcriptions:
Adler, *Handbuch*, vol. 1, p.190.
Davidson and Apel, *Historical*, vol. 1, p.16.
Hamburg, *Muziekgeschiedenis*, p.11.
Husmann, "Kalenda Maya," p.277.
Leuchter, *Florilegium*, p.9.
McPeek, "Kalenda Maia," p.147.
McPeek, "Medieval Monophonic Song," p.5.
Werf, "Estampie," p.255.

No.1b. Souvent Souspire   vocal estampie

Counting unit: ♩.
Principal source of music and text: Paris, Bibl. l'Arsenal MS 5198, pp.332–33.
Other sources:
Paris, BN, fonds français, 845, f. 159v–160r.
Paris, BN, fonds français, 847, f. 136r–v.
Paris, BN, Nouv. Acq. 1050, f. 208r–09r.
    All four manuscripts are major sources of the trouvère repertory, dating from the fourteenth century. The author of the text is not known.
    Similar to that of No.1a, the notation consists mostly of longas with a few ligatures, and the transcription has been made according to the same principles. As in "Kalenda Maya," the final section of the first verse text is editorially marked to serve as a refrain. Text transcription and translation by Robert Taylor.

Facsimile:
Aubry, *Le Chansonnier de l'Arsenal*, p.332–33.

Transcription:
Husmann, "Kalenda Maya," p.276.

No.2   [nota or estampie]

Counting unit: ♩.
Unique source: Oxford, Bodleian Library, Douce 139, fol. 5v.
    A manuscript from the thirteenth century containing numerous English statutes, many referring to Coventry, is the probable origin of the manuscript.
    The notation allows both a mensural and a modal rhythm transcription. A mensural transcription results in duple rhythm with duple subdivision, e.g., ♩♫♩♫. Modal rhythm yields a similar duple rhythm, but with triple subdivision, either mode 3 ♩. ♪ ♩♪ ♩ or alternate mode 3 ♩. ♩♪ ♩. ♩♪. Ernest Sanders has discussed the problem in detail, and the transcription in this edition follows his suggestion of alternate mode 3.[5]
    At the end of *partes* 1, 2, 3, and 5, there is a double bar followed by an additional note and four bars, e.g.,‖¶ ‖‖. In every case the last two notes have the same pitch and durational value, and I have interpreted this to be the scribe's method of indicating repetition of the *pars*. At the end of *pars* 7 there is only one final note, a maxima with what apears to be a correction: ♯‖‖. It is not clear whether the scribe was adding or deleting the repeat mark, and I have indicated this by enclosing the repeat mark in parentheses.
    The first ten bars of *pars* 9 are copied out of place in the manuscript but marked by a "+" in the margin for correct placement. The last eight bars of *pars* 6 are also copied out of place, following the polyphonic section of *pars* 10, but are not indicated as such in the manuscript. I have placed it according to the pattern in every other section in which two similar phrases follow one another.

Two possible performance sequences are suggested and discussed above, p.13:

1. As a nota, performed exactly as edited.
2. As an estampie, by repeating every *pars* and performing the polyphonic section of *pars* 10 as a refrain at the end of each one.

Facsimiles:
Arlt, "Instrumentalmusik."
Stainer, *Early*, vol. 1, Plate 7.
Wooldridge, *Early*, vol. 1, Plate 24.

Transcriptions:
Davidson and Apel, *Historical*, vol. 1, p.43.
Handschin, "Über Estampie," pp.13–14.
Sanders, "Duple Rhythm," pp.289–91.
Wolf, *Handbuch*, vol. 1, pp.234–35.
Wolf, "Die Tänze," pp.22–23.

Nos.3–13

Unique source: Paris, Bibliothèque Nationale, fonds français 844, fols. 5r, 103v–104v.

The manuscript dates from the second half of the thirteenth century and is known as "Chansonnier du Roi." It contains trouvère repertory as well as a few troubadour songs. Several pages have been partially cut away, probably in order to remove the illuminated initials. It is in this way that the first several *partes* of No. 3 have been lost.

The transcription here is according to mensural notation.[6] This is basically the system used by Pierre Aubry, although he selected a triple subdivision relating the notation more closely with rhythmic modal values, and I have selected the duple subdivision of the later mensural system.

The scribe has used a dot to mark off perfections and to prevent imperfections in ambiguous places. All *partes* have been transcribed beginning on the downbeat except for those places where an incomplete measure is followed by a unit of 3 b's, for example, the beginning of No.8, *pars* 1.

Facsimiles:
Aubry, *Estampies*.
Beck, *Le Manuscrit*, vol. 1.
Die Musik in Geschichte und Gegenwart, vol. 3, cols. 1553–54 [Nos.6–11].
Werf, "Estampie," p.255.

Transcriptions:
Aubry, *Estampies*, pp.13–24.
Davidson and Apel, *Historical*, vol.1, pp.42–43 [Nos.6, 13].
Gleason, *Examples*, p.57 [No.13].
Hoppin, *Anthology*, p.118 [No.11].
Keruzoré, *Estampies*.
Reichert, *Der Tanz*, p.17 [No.8].
Werf, "Estampie," p.254 [No.4].

No.3. [La Prime Estampie Royal] fol. 103v   estampie

The title and the first several *partes* have been cut away. Cues at the end of the two remaining *partes* indicate only the first three notes of the *ouvert* ending.

No.4. La Seconde Estampie Royal fol. 103v, 104r   estampie

Counting unit: ♩.

Ouvert and *clos* are given at the end of *pars* 1 and are indicated by cue for *partes* 2, 3, and 6. No indication for *pars* 4. After eight measure *pars* 5 has 3 sb *a*, *b*, *a*, at the end of the line, which in all other editions have been transcribed at face value with the next line considered to be a continuation of the same *pars*. I have interpreted the three notes as a cue to the first ending but with the second and third notes written a step too low. As a result of this reading the following line has been treated as an additional *pars*. Supporting evidence for this reading is that all other *partes* are only one manuscript line long, and the fact that they all fall into two clear subphrases rather than the four that would result if the two lines were considered to be a single *pars*.

No.5. *La Tierche Estampie Roial* fol. 104r   estampie

Counting unit: ♩.
   Ouvert and *clos* given at the end of *pars* 1 and indicated by cue for all remaining *partes*.

No.6, *La Quarte Estampie Royal* fol. 104r   estampie

Counting unit: ♩.
   Ouvert and *clos* given at the end of *pars* 1 and indicated by cue for all remaining *partes*.
   1st *pars*: opening ligature bb transcribed as altered.
   6th *pars*: dot of perfection missing after n.4.

No.7. *La Quinte Estampie Real* fol. 104v   estampie

Counting unit: ♩.
   Endings written out in each *pars*.

No.8. *La Seste Estampie Real* fol 104v   estampie

Counting unit: ♩.
   Endings written out in each *pars*.

No.9. *La Septime Estampie Real* fol. 104v   estampie

Counting unit: ♩.
   Endings written out in each *pars*.
   4th *pars*: detached single b at beginning suggests possible interpretation as an upbeat pattern, but this would require alteration of n.8.

No.10. *La Uitime Estampie Real* fol. 104v   estampie

Counting unit: ♩.
   Endings written out in each *pars*.
   Dot of perfection prevents transcription of the endings beginning on an upbeat and requires imperfection on the penultimate note of the *clos* endings.

No.11. *Dansse Real* fol 104v   [ductia]

Counting unit: ♩.
   Ouvert and *clos* endings are not marked in the manuscript. They are added here according to Grocheio's statement that all dances have double *puncta*. The manuscript shows signs of erasures and corrections for the endings of each of the *partes*.

No.12   fol. 5r   [ductia]

Counting unit: ♩
Ouvert and *clos* are given at the end of *pars* 1 and are indicated by cue for all remaining *partes.*

No.13. Danse   fol. 5r   [ductia]

Counting unit: ♩
Ouvert and *clos* are given at the end of *pars* 1 and are indicated by cue for the remaining *partes.*

Nos.14–28
Unique source: London, British Library, Additional 29987 fols. 55v–63v.

Gilbert Reaney dates the manuscript between the late 1390s and the early years of the fifteenth century in northern Italy.[7] Kurt von Fischer further identifies it as associated with the Visconti family in Milan on the basis of the names of two of the dances: "Principio de Virtu" (No.21), which he connects with Gian Galeazzo Visconti, Conte di Virtù; and "Isabella" (No.16), the name of Gian Galeazzo's first wife (died 1372).[8] I have suggested that, in addition, the dance names "Ghaetta" (No.14) and "Belicha" (No.18) may be evidence of some contact with the southern area of Italy near Naples.[9]

The manuscript contains 119 compositions, all of them fourteenth-century Italian, including ballatas, madrigals, caccias, three Mass sections, a hymn, these fifteen dances, and the "Chançoneta tedescha" tenors, Nos.35–38. The composers of the dances and some of the vocal music are unknown, but 80 of the vocal works have been identified as the music of Francesco Landini, Niccolo da Perugia, Jacopo da Bologna, and various less-known Italian composers of the fourteenth century.[10] The dances appear in the middle of the manuscript, interrupted by two ballatas inserted after the *prima pars* of "Belicha."

The notation is that of the Italian trecento: quaternaria, signified by ꝗ when not obvious; senaria imperfecta, signified by "s.i." when not obvious; and ternaria, signified by ꝉ. The signs for repetition of sections are not always complete or clear. The scribe has used a complex system of marks—circles, hand with pointing finger, helmet, Maltese cross, etc.—in order to avoid writing out the repeated material from *pars* to *pars*, but in some cases he has failed to complete the markings. There are several obvious errors, only some of which have been corrected in the manuscript by the scribe. The entire section in the manuscript is marked "Istanpitta" at the top of the first page on which the dances appear, and the name of each dance is written under the first line of music, with the first letter of the name marked in the margin for illumination that was never completed.

Facsimiles:
Gushee, "Analytical," pp.181–84 [Nos.14–16].
Reaney, *The Manuscript.*
Stäblein, *Schriftbild*, p.177 [Nos.23, 26].
Ulsamer and Stahmer, *Musikalisches*, p.10 [No.23].

Transcriptions:
Bokum, *De dansen.*
Caldwell, *Medieval*, p.111 [No.23].
Crane, "On Performing," p.24 [No.27].
Davidson and Apel, *Historical*, pp.63–64 [Nos.25, 27].
Gleason, *Examples*, p.57 [No.22].
Godwin, *Schirmer*, p.56 [No.23].
Hamburg, *Muziekgeschiedenis*, p.46 [Nos.27].

Harriman, *Monophonic* [Nos.14–19, 22–28].
Hoppin, *Anthology*, p.119 [No.26].
Kahl, *Das Charakterstück*, p.19 [Nos.27].
Kelber and Ulsamer, *Mittelalterliche*.
Lerner, *Study*, p.45 [No.24].
Leuchter, *Florilegium*, p.37 [No.23].
Marrocco and Sandon, *Medieval*, pp.196–98 [Nos.15, 24].
Moser, "Stantipes," pp.196–206 [Nos.14, 16, 23, 27, 28].
Reichert, *Der Tanz*, p.27 [Nos.24, 26].
Schering, *Geschichte*, pp.20–22 [Nos.24, 27, 28].
Stäblein, *Schriftbild*, p.176 [No.23].
Ulsamer and Stahmer, *Musikalisches*, p.11 [No.23].
Werf, "Estampie," pp.256–57 [No.16].
Wolf, "Die Tänze," pp.10–42.

No.14. *Ghaetta* fol. *55v–56r* estampie

Name: possibly the city of Gaeta near Naples, and the Spanish word for bagpipe.
Counting unit: ♩·
Notation: senaria imperfecta, quaternaria

No.15. *Chominciamento di gioia* fol. *56r, v* estampie

Name: "The beginning of joy"
Counting unit: ♩·
Notation: senaria imperfecta
   Terza pars, bar 11, n.4, sm.
   Quarta pars, from beginning to square bracket, a third too high in the manuscript, confirmed by the cues for repeat at the end of both the *quarta* and *quinta partes*.
   Bar 3, n. 1 missing.
   Quinta pars, bar 13, n.1, sm.

No.16. *Isabella* fol. *56v, 57r* estampie

Name: a common Italian first name
Counting unit: ♩
   The opening bars of this dance consist of only a single note, played at decreasing durations. The performer may wish to elaborate on this by incorporating it into a prelude, extending the phrase, and gradually increasing the speed of the single note until it reaches tempo.
Notation: quaternaria, ternaria
   Secunda pars, all notes in the seven bars before the square bracket are a third too high in the manuscript.

No.17. *Tre fontane* fol. *57r, v* estampie

Name: "three fountains"
Counting unit: ♩
Notation: quaternaria, senaria imperfecta

No.18. *Belicha* fol. *58r, 59v* estampie

Name: could be the Italian word for "war" (bellico), or the Arabic word "billiq," a popular comic and licentious poem.[11]
Counting unit: ♩
Notation: quaternaria, senaria imperfecta

Written at the end of the *prima pars* is "il avanço di questa istampita enne inaçi a charte 196 a questo segnno ⊢♀⊣" (The remainder of this estampie is found on page 196 at this sign ⊢♀⊣). Folios 58v and 59r contain two ballatas, and "Belicha" resumes at the top of fol. 59v. (The pages have several sets of numbers. Obviously at one time the manuscript was much longer).

Terza pars, bar 8, n.5 m.

Quarta pars, bar 43, additional sb on "d."

No.19. Parlamento   fol. 60r, v   estampie

Name: "dialogue"
Counting unit: ♩.
Notation: senaria imperfecta

Secunda pars, bar 7, sb rest.

Quarta pars, *aperto* not marked. Selection has been made because of agreement with the beginning of the *chiuso*.

No.20. In Pro   fol. 60v, 61r   estampie

Name: an old form of "per favore" (please)
Counting unit: ♩
Notation: quaternaria, senaria imperfecta

Terza pars, custos indicates notes in bars 15–17 should be a third higher than written in the manuscript.

No.21. Principio di virtu   fol. 61r–62r   estampie

Name: "principle of virtue"
Counting unit: ♩
Notation: quaternaria

No.22. Salterello   fol. 62r   saltarello

Counting unit: ♩.
Notation: senaria imperfecta

Prima pars, three bars before end of *aperto*, additional sm *f*, *g* at beginning of group.

Quarta pars, bar 23, additional sm *f*, *g*, *a* at beginning of group.

No.23. Salterello   fol. 62v   saltarello

Counting unit: ♩
Notation: quaternaria

No.24. Salterello   fol. 62v, 63r   saltarello

Counting unit: ♩.
Notation: senaria imperfecta

Secunda pars is missing from source.

No.25. Salterello   fol. 63v   saltarello

Counting unit: ♩
Notation: quaternaria

No.26. Trotto   fol. 62v   trotto

Counting unit: ♩.
Notation: senaria imperfecta

Secunda pars, bar 9 appears to be a bar and a half. This is unusual because the notation system is based on the division of a whole unit of measure. The presence of the same material in the *terza pars* suggests that it is not an error. The extra-long measure is the solution arrived at by R. Hoppin.[12]

No.27. *Lamento di Tristano, La rotta* fol. 63r   estampie and rotta

Counting unit: ♩
Notation: quaternaria
Rotta *secunda pars* music has been omitted from the source, and only the endings are included. The reconstruction is that proposed by F. Crane and is used by permission.[13]

No.28. *La Manfredina, La Rotta della Manfredina* fol. 63v   estampie and rotta

Counting unit: ♩
Notation: quaternaria

No.29. *Dança Amorosa, Troto*   estampie and troto

Name: amorous dance
Counting unit: ♩
Unique source: Florence, Archivio di Stato, Notarile Antecosimiano No. 17879 (unnumbered folios). Title written "Danança Amorosa" in manuscript.
The archival source is a notarial record from 1380 to 1450, mostly written by the notary Bartolomeo di Franco Ridolfi. The dances are on the back of a loose piece of paper used to register land transfer and dated 22 March, 1389 [1390 in modern terms]. The notation is Italian trecento.
Dança, second ending written at end of third *pars*, and indicated by sign (pointing finger) in each *pars*.
Prima pars, first ending, n.6 sm., penultimate note "g."
Troto, *chiuso* written at the end of first *pars* and indicated by sign in all *partes*. *Terza pars*, final note missing.

Facsimile and Transcription:
McGee, " 'Dança Amorosa': A Newly-discovered Medieval Dance Pair."

No.30. *Czaldy Waldy*   [Tenors]

Counting unit: ♩
Primary source: Prague, Czechoslovakia State Library MS XVII F9.
Other source: Prague, Czechoslovakia State Library MS XIV D 23.
The notation is black breves and semibreves, with dots over the breves signifying duple length. The title "Czaldy Waldy" appears only at the beginning of the second melody in the principal source, whereas the concordant manuscript contains only the second melody, but without a title. According to Václav Plocek, neither source can be exactly dated. He dates XVII F9 from the late fourteenth or early fifteenth century, and XIV D 23 from slightly earlier.[14]
Second piece, n.13 sb

Facsimile and Transcription:
Plocek, "K problematice," pp.5–10.

Nos.31–34

Unique source: Montpellier, Bibliothèque de l'Ecole de Médecine H 196.
The manuscript was copies in the last third of the thirteenth century and comprises a number of layers of material in the hands of numerous scribes and in a variety of

early notational systems. It is one of the largest early sources of motets, containing 336 polyphonic compositions, all but eight with music.

Facsimile:
Rokseth, *Polyphonies du XIIIe siecle*, vol. I, fols. 299r–300v, 333v–35r, 336v–37v, 339v–41r.

Transcriptions:
Rokseth, *Polyphonies du XIIIe siecle*, vol. 3, 118–20 [No.31], 168–69 [No.32], 172–73 [No.33], 176–78 [No.34].
Wolf, "Die Tänze," p.22.

No.31. Chose Tassin [1]   fol. 299r–300v
Tenor for motet *Amours dont je sai/L'autrier au douz mois d'Avril/Chose Tassin*.
Counting unit: ♩.

No.32. Chose Tassin [2]   fol. 333v–35r
 Tenor for motet *De chanter me vient Talens/Bien doi boine/Chose Tassin*
Counting unit: ♩.

No.33. Chose Tassin [3]   fol. 336v–38r
 Tenor for motet *Entre Jehan et Philippet/Nus hom ne puet desiervir/Chose Tassin*.
Counting unit: ♩.

No.34. Chose Loyset   fol. 339v–41v
 Tenor for motet *Quant che vient/Mout ai esté longuement/Chose Loyset*.
Counting unit: ♩.
 In transcriptions of the three-part motet, rests are added at the ends of the first two sections in order to allow the tenor to correspond with the duplum and the triplum.

Nos.35–38
Unique source: London, British Library, Additional 29987, fol. 74
 See description of manuscript for Nos.14–28 above. All compositions are in black breves and semibreves and are in two *partes*. They may be bassadanza tenors.

Facsimiles:
Arlt, "Instrumentalmusik."
Reaney, *The Manuscript*.

No.35. Chançoneta Tedescha [1]   Tenor
Counting unit: ♩

No.36. Chançona Tedescha [2]   Tenor
Counting unit: ♩

No.37. Chançona Tedescha [3]   Tenor
Counting unit: ♩

No.38. Chançona Tedescha [4]   Tenor
Counting unit: ♩

Nos.39–41
Unique source: London, British Library, Harley 978 fol. 8v, 9r.
 This miscellaneous English manuscript from the late thirteenth century contains

five musical compositions, including the rota "Sumer is icumen in." The music is in modal notation. All three compositions are basically in mode 1 with subdivisions.

Facsimilies:
Apel, *The Notation*, p.239 [fol. 9r].
Wolf, *Handbuch*, vol. 1, p.224.
Wooldridge, *Early*, vol. 1, Plates 18, 19.

Transcriptions:
Davidson and Apel, *Historical*, vol. 1, pp.43–44 [Nos.39, 40].
Parrish and Ohl, *Master*, pp.33–35 [No.41].
Reichert, *Der Tanz*, p.17 [No.41].
Sanders, *Polyphonic*, pp.24–26.
Wolf, *Handbuch*, vol. 1, pp.224–27 [No.39].
Wolf, "Die Tänze," pp.39–42.

No.39   fol. 8v, 9r   [nota]

Counting unit: ♩
   The two parts are written one after the other.

No.40   fol. 9r   [nota]

Counting unit: ♩
   The two parts are written in score format, more or less aligned.

No.41   fol. 9r   [nota]

Counting unit: ♩
   The two parts are in score format but the alignment is not close.
   Bar 12 superior: extra *d*, *e* at end.
   Bars 33, 34, 37, 38 superior are obviously ornamented versions of corresponding sections in the fourth *pars*, but it is not clear from the notation which beat is to be subdivided.

Nos.42–44
Unique source: London, British Library, Additional 28550 (Robertsbridge Codex), fol. 43r, v.
   The manuscript proper contains a chronicle of several English abbeys, including Robertsbridge, all from the early fourteenth century. Bound in at the end of the chronicle are two folios of music, which include the intabulation of two motets also found in the *Romas de Fauvel* and possibly by Philippe di Vitry, an anonymous hymn, and the three untexted compositions edited here. In private correspondence Margaret Bent has kindly provided the opinion that the musical notation is probably English and from the last third of the fourteenth century.
   The pages are somewhat mutilated, and the notes are difficult to decipher. The notation is commonly referred to as keyboard tablature–a combination of neumes for the upper voice and letters for the lower. The intended performance medium may have been, in addition to keyboard, duets such as lute and harp, lute and vielle, or two lutes.[15]

Facsimiles:
Apel, *The Notation*, p.38 [No.44].
Arlt, "Instrumentalmusik" [No.44].
Die Musik in Geschichte und Gegenwart, vol. 3, cols. 1557–58; Tafel 25 [No.44].
Parrish, *The Notation*, Plate LXI [Nos.42, 43].
Wolf, *Handbuch*, vol. 2, p.9.
Wooldridge, *Early*, vol. 1, plates 42, 43.

Transcriptions:
Apel, *Keyboard.*
Davidson and Apel, *Historical,* vol. 1, pp.62–63 [No.43].
Handschin, "Über," pp.14–18 [Nos.43–44].
Sanders, Harrison, Lefferts, eds., *English Music,* pp.149–55.
Wolf, *Handbuch,* vol. 2, pp.9–10 [No.44 partial].

No.42 (fragment)   fol. 43r

Not enough remains of this composition to identify it. See pp. 17–18 above.

No.43   fol. 43r   [estampie]

Counting unit: ♩.

No.44. Petrone   fol. 43v   [estampie]

Counting unit: ♩.
There has been some controversy over this title; the other common reading is "Retrove." I have adopted the reading of Frederick Crane, although I am not convinced, as he is, that this is the ductia "Pierron" referred to by Grocheio in reference to ductias with four *puncta.*[16]
  Clos ending, bar 1, after n.4 additional m e, d, e, c.
  Secundus Punctus, bar 3, 4 m, 2 sb.
  Quintus Punctus, bar 1, n.4 and 5, 2 sb; bar 3, b.

Nos.45–47

Unique source: Faenza, Biblioteca Comunale 117 (Faenza Codex) fols. 52v–56v, 80v–81r
There is some disagreement as to the exact date of this manuscript. Dragan Plamenac places it from the early years of the fifteenth century; Michael Kugler suggests ca. 1430; but see my suggestion of a possible slightly later date of ca. 1435–40.[17] In addition to the three dances edited here, the manuscript includes elaborately ornamented intabluations of sacred works and French and Italian secular vocal music from the late fourteenth century. The notation is Italian, in score format.
The names "Tumpes" and "Sangilio" are readings by Plamenac of almost indecipherable marginal markings. He speculates that they may not be the titles of the dances. Adriano Cavicchi suggests that two of the dance names indicate a connection with the court at Ferrara. He points out that "Belfiore" was the name of the Ferrara palace constructed in 1390–92, and that "Sangilio" may be Ferrarese dialect for Sant' Egidio, a place near Ferrara, or S[ignor]a Gilio[la], referring to the wife of Nicolò III of Ferrara.[18]
There has been controversy as to the instrument(s) for which the Faenza material was composed and a proposal that the manuscript was originally intended for two lutes or lute and vielle.[19]

Facsimile:
Carapetyan, *An Early.*

Transcriptions:
Huestis, *Transcriptions.*
Plamenac, *Keyboard.*

No.45. Tumpes (Ms: Tüpes)   fol. 52v–54r   [estampie]

Meaning of the title is obscure.
Counting unit: ♩
The separate *partes* are marked off by double and quadruple bar lines. The sign "C," found in *prima pars* bar 78, is interpreted as meaning a refrain. I have therefore

added the section from that point to the end of the *pars* at the end of both the second and third *partes*. The sign "C" occurs again at the end of the *quarta pars* with "+," which I have interpreted as meaning that the music from this point on is a written-out variation of the refrain.

No.46. Sangilio   fol. 54v–56v   [estampie]

For possible meaning of the name see above.
Counting unit: ♩

In the *prima pars* after bar 26 there are fifteen bars erroneously copied from another work.[20] The separate *partes* are marked off by double bars. As in "Tumpes," signs in the manuscript have been interpreted as references to the repetition of endings.

In the *quarta pars*, no marks are given for the endings. The separation here and identification as *ouvert* and *clos* endings are conjectures based on the similarity between the music found in these two places with that marked as the cue to the endings in earlier *partes*. The final ending is a bit abrupt, and it is possible that the second ending material from the *prima pars* was intended but that the scribe was confused by the signs and added the final cadence measure.

No.47. Bel fiore dança   fol. 80v–81r   [bassadanza]

Title: Beautiful flower, dance
Counting unit: ♩

NOTES

1. Elizabeth Aubrey, "The Transmission of Troubadour Melodies: The Testimony of Paris, Bibliothèque nationale, f. fr. 22543," *Text* 3 (1987):213.

2. See, for example, Pierre Aubry, *Trouvères et Troubadours* (New York and London, 1914; reprint, New York, 1969); Jean Beck, *Die Melodien der Troubadours* (Strasbourg, 1908), English translation, T. Wardell, *The Music of the Troubadours* (Santa Barbara, 1979).

3. See Gwynn S. McPeek, "Medieval Monophonic Song; *Kalenda Maia* by Raimbault de Vaqueiras 9c.1155–105," in *Notations and Editions: a Book in Honor of Louise Cuyler*, edited by Edith Borroff (Dubuque: Brown, 1974); Hendrik van der Werf, "The Trouvère Chansons as Creations of a Notationless Culture," *Current Musicology* I (1965):61–82; Werf, "Concerning the Measurability of Medieval Music," *Current Musicology* X (1970):69–73; Werf, "Deklamatorischer Rhythmus in den Chansons der Trouveres," *Musikforschung* XX (1967):122–44; Friedrich Gennrich, "Die Deutungen der Rhythmik der Kalenda-maya-melodie," *Festschrift für Gerhard Rohlfs* (Halle, 1958), pp.181–92. See also the Introduction by Alejandro Planchart in the English translation of Beck, *The Music*.

4. See discussion in Timothy J. McGee, "Medieval Dances: Matching the Repertory with Grocheio's Descriptions," *The Journal of Musicology* 7 (1989):498–517.

5. Ernest Sanders, "Duple Rhythm and Alternate Third Mode in the 13th Century," *Journal of the American Musicological Society* 15 (1962).

6. Hendrik van der Werf also believes that the notation is mensural, see "Estampie," *The New Grove*, vol. 6, p.254.

7. Gilbert Reaney, *The Manuscript British Museum Additional 29987* (Rome, 1965), p.8.

8. Kurt von Fischer, "Ein Versuch sur chronologie von Landinis Werken," *Musica Disciplina* XX (1966):38. This replaces his earlier identification of the manuscript as from Perugia, in *Studien zur italienischen Musik des Trecento und frühen Quattrocento* (Bern, 1956), p.92.

9. Timothy J. McGee, "Eastern Influences in Medieval European Dances," in *Cross-*

Cultural Perspectives on Music, edited by Robert Falck and Timothy Rice (Toronto: University of Toronto Press, 1982), p.98.

   10. See inventory in Reaney, *The Manuscript*, pp.18–26.

   11. McGee, "Eastern Influences," p.98.

   12. Richard Hoppin, *Anthology of Medieval Music* (New York: W. W. Norton, 1978), p.119.

   13. Frederick Crane, "On Performing the Lo Estampies," *Early Music* VII (1979):24, 26.

   14. See Václav Plocek, "K problematice nasich nejstarsich tanecnich skladeb," *Hudebni Veda* 6 (1969):3–25; Plocek, "Jeste k problematice Czaldy waldy," *Hudebni Veda* 7 (1970):46–57; and Plocek, "Zur Problematik der ältesten tschechischen Tanzkompositionen," *Studia Musicologica* 13 (1971):241–47.

   15. See Timothy J. McGee, "Instruments and the Faenza Codex," *Early Music* 14 (1986):486–88.

   16. Ernst Rohloff, *Die quellenhandschriften zum Musiktraktat des Johannes de Grocheio* (Leipzig: Deutscher Verlag, 1972), p.136; Albert Seay, *Johannes De Grocheio Concerning Music* (Colorado Springs: Colorado College of Music Press, 1973), p.21. See Frederick Crane, "A Study of Theoretical Writings on Musical Form to ca. 1460," Ph.D. diss., University of Iowa, 1960.

   17. Dragan Plamanac, *Keyboard Music of the Late Middle Ages in Codex Faenza 117* (Rome: American Institute of Musicology, 1972); Michael Kugler, *Die Tastenmusik im Codex Faenza*, Munchner Veröffentlichungen zur Musikgeschichte, Band 21, edited by T. G. Georgiades (Tutzing: Hans Schneider, 1972), p.51; McGee, "Instruments and the Faenza Codex," p.486.

   18. Adriano Cavicchi, "Sacro e profano. Documenti e note su Bartolomeo da Bologna e gli organisti della cattedrale di Ferrara nel primo Quattrocento," *Revue Italiana di Musicologia* X (1975):70. See the additional suggestion of Ferrara as the place of origin and a possible connection between the manuscript and the famous lutenist Pietrobono de Burzellis in McGee, "Instruments and the Faenza Codex."

   19. See McGee, "Instruments and the Faenza Codex."

   20. See G. Reaney, review in *Journal of the American Musicological Society* 29 (1976):141.

Facsimiles and Transcriptions

The following is a list of all facsimiles and transcriptions of the medieval instrumental dance repertory known to this writer.

facs. = facsimile
trans. = transcriptions
The numbers indicate which pieces in the present edition are contained in the source.

Adler, Guido. *Handbuch der Musikgeschichte.* 2 vols. Berlin: H. Keller, 1924; reprint Tutzing, 1961. Vol. 1, p.190, trans. No.1a.

Apel, Willi, ed. *Keyboard Music of the Fourteenth and Fifteenth Centuries.* Corpus of Early Keyboard Music, vol. 1. Rome: American Institute of Musicology, 1963. Pp.1–3, trans. Nos.42–44.

————. *The Notation of Polyphonic Music 900–1600.* 5th ed. Cambridge: Medieval Academy of America, 1953. P.239, facs. No.39 lower voice, Nos.40, 41; p.38, No.44.

Arlt, Wilf. "Instrumentalmusik im mittelalter: Fragen der Rekonstruktion einer schriftlosen Praxis," *Basler Jahrbuch für Historische Musikpraxis* 7 (1983):47, 51, 60, facs. Nos.35–38, 2, 44.

Aubry, Pierre. *Le Chansonnier de l'Arsenal.* Paris: Paul Geuthner, n.d. Pp.332–33, facs. No.1b.

————. *Estampies et danses Royales, Les plus anciens textes de musique instrumentale du Moyen-Age.* Paris, 1907; reprint Geneva: Minkoff, 1975. After p.12, facs. and trans. Nos.3–13.

Beck, Jean, ed. *Le Manuscrit du Roi, Fonds Français No 844 de la Bibliothèque Nationale.* 2 vols. Philadelphia, 1938; reprint New York: Broude Bros., 1970. Vol.1, facs. Nos.3–13.

Bokum, Jan ten, ed. *De dansen van het trecento.* Scripta musicologica ultrajectina. Utrecht: Instituut voor Muziekwetenshap der Rijksuniversiteit, 1967; 2d ed., 1976, trans. Nos.14–28.

Caldwell, John. *Medieval Music.* Bloomington: Indiana University Press, 1978. P.111, trans. No.23.

Carapetyan, Armen, ed. *An Early Fifteenth-Century Italian Source of Keyboard Music: The Codex Faenza, Biblioteca Comunale, 117.* Musicological Studies and Documents #10. Rome: American Institute of Musicology, 1961. Facs. Nos.45–47.

Crane, Frederick. "On performing the Lo Estampies," *Early Music* VII (1979):24, trans. No.27.

Davison, Archibald, and Willi Apel. *Historical Anthology of Music.* Rev. ed., 2 vols. Cambridge: Harvard University Press, 1950. Vol. 1, *Oriental, Medieval and Renaissance Music,* pp.16, 42–44, 62–64; trans. Nos.1a, 2, 6, 13, 25, 27, 39, 40, 43.

Gleason, Harold, ed. *Examples of Music Before 1400.* Rev. ed. Eastman School of Music Series 10. Rochester: Eastman School of Music, 1946. P.57, trans. Nos.13, 22.

Godwin, Joscelyn, ed. *Schirmer Scores.* New York: G. Schirmer, 1975. P.56, trans. No.23.

Gushee, Lawrence. "Analytical Method and Compositional Process in Some Thirteenth- and Fourteenth-Century Music," *Aktuelle Fragen der Musikbezogenen Mittelalterforschung,* Forum musicologicum III, 1975. Pp.181–84, facs. Nos.14–16.

Hamburg, Otto. *Muziekgeschiedenis in voorbeelden.* Utrecht, 1973. English translation, Susan Hellauer, *Music History in Examples.* Wilhelmshaven: Heinrichshofen, 1978. Pp.11, 46, trans. Nos.1a, 27.

Handschin, Jacques. "Über Estampie und Sequenz," *Zeitschrift für Musikwissenschaft* XII (1929):13–18, trans. Nos.2, 43–44.

Harriman, Ralph, ed. *Monophonic Dances of the 14th Century.* San Lorenzo, California: Musica Sacra et Profana, 1976. Trans. Nos.14–19, 22–28.

Hoppin, Richard, ed. *Anthology of Medieval Music.* New York: W. W. Norton, 1978. P.119, trans. Nos.11, 26.

Huestis, Robert, ed. *Transcriptions from the Faenza Codex.* N.p. 1971. Pp.80–88, 119–120, trans. Nos.45–47.

Husmann, Heinrich. "Kalenda Maya," *Archiv für Musikwissenschaft* X (1953):276–77, trans. Nos.1a, 1b.

Kahl, Willi, ed. *Das Charakterstück.* Das Musikwerk 8. Cologne: Arno Volk, 1955. English ed., *The Character Piece*, Anthology of Music 8, 1961. P.19, trans. No.27.

Kelber, Sebastian, and Josef Ulsamer. *Mittelalterliche Spielmannstänze aus Italien.* Das Blockflöten Repertoire. 2 vol. Vol. 1, Celle: Moeck Verlag, 1978, trans. Nos.14–17, 22, 23, 26; vol. 2, in press, trans. Nos.18–21, 24, 25, 27–28.

Keruzoré, Alain. *Estampies et Danses Royales.* Paris, 1973. Trans. Nos.3–13.

Lerner, Edward R., ed. *Study Scores of Musical Styles.* New York, 1968. P.45, trans. No.24.

Leuchter, Erwin, ed. *Florilegium Musicum.* Buenos Aires, 1964. Pp.9, 37, trans. Nos.1a, 23.

McGee, Timothy J. " 'Dança Amorosa': A Newly-discovered Medieval Dance Pair." In *Festschrift for Luther Dittmer.* Ottawa: Institute for Mediaeval Music, 1990.

McPeek, Gwynn S. "Kalenda Maia: A Study in Form." In *Medieval Studies in Honor of Robert White Linker.* N.p.: Editorial Castalia, 1973. P.147, trans. No.1a.

———."Medieval Monophonic Song; *Kalenda Maia* by Raimbault de Vaqueiras (c.1155–1205)." In *Notations and Editions: a Book in Honor of Louise Cuyler,* edited by Edith Borroff. Dubuque: Brown, 1974. Pp.3, 5, facs. and trans. No.1a.

Marrocco, W. Thomas, and Nicholas Sandon, eds. *Medieval Music, The Oxford Anthology of Music.* London: Oxford University Press, 1977. Pp.196–98, trans. Nos.15, 24.

Moser, Hans Joachim. "Stantipes and Ductia," *Zeitschrift für Musikwissenschaft* 2 (1919–20):194–206, trans. Nos.14, 16, 23, 27, 28.

Die Musik in Geschichte und Gegenwart. Kassel and Basel: Bärenreiter. Vol. III, 1954, Cols. 1553–54, facs. Nos.6–11, Cols. 1557–58, facs. No.44. Vol. XI, 1963, Tafel 25, facs. No.44.

Parrish, Carl. *The Notation of Medieval Music.* New York: W. W. Norton, 1959; reprint New York: Pendragon Press, 1978. Plate LXI, facs. Nos.42, 43.

Parrish, Carl, and John F. Ohl. *Masterpieces of Music Before 1750: An Anthology of Musical Examples from Gregorian Chant to J. S. Bach.* New York: W. W. Norton, 1951. Pp.34–35, trans. No.41.

Plamenac, Dragan, ed. *Keyboard Music of the Late Middle Ages in Codex Faenza 117.* Rome: American Institute of Musicology, 1972. Pp.53–59, 102, trans. Nos.45–47.

Plocek, Václav. "K problematice nasich nystarsich tanecnich skladeb," *Hudebni Veda* 6 (1969):5–6, 6–8, facs. and trans. No.30.

Reaney, Gilbert, ed. *The Manuscript London, British Museum, Additional 29987, A Facsimile Edition.* Musicological Studies and Documents #13. Rome: American Institute of Musicology, 1965. Facs. Nos.14–28, 35–38.

Reichert, George, ed. *Der Tanz.* Das Musikwerk 27. Cologne: Arno Volk, 1965. English ed., *The Dance*, Anthology of Music 27, 1974. P.17, trans. Nos.8, 24, 26, 41.

Rokseth, Yvonne, ed. *Polyphonies du XIIIe siecle: Le manuscrit H 196 de la Faculté de Médecine du Montpellier.* 4 vols. Paris: L'Oiseau Lyre, 1935. Vol. I, Fols. 299r–300v, 333v–35r, 336v–37v, 339v–41r, facs.Nos.31–34. Vol. III, pp.118–20, 168–69, 172–73, 176–78, trans. Nos.31–34.

Sanders, Ernest. "Duple Rhythm and Alternate Third Mode in the 13th Century," *Journal of the American Musicological Society* XV (1962):189–91, trans. No.2.

Sanders, Ernest, ed. *English Music of the Thirteenth and Early Fourteenth Centuries.* Polyphonic Music of the Fourteenth Century, edited by Kurt von Fischer assisted by Ian Bent. Vol. XIV, Monaco: L'Oiseau Lyre, 1979, pp.24–26, trans. Nos.39–41.

Sanders, Ernest H., Frank Ll. Harrison, and Peter Lefferts, eds. *English Music of the Thirteenth and Early Fourteenth Centuries,* edited by Kurt von Fischer assisted by Ian Bent. Vol. XVII, Monaco: L'Oiseau Lyre, 1986. Pp.149–55, trans. Nos.42–44.

Schering, Arnold, ed. *Geschichte der Musik in Beispielen.* Leipzig, 1931; reprint New York, 1950. Pp.20–22, trans. No.24, 27, 28.

Stäblein, Bruno. *Schriftbild der einstimmigen Musik.* Musikgeschichte in Bildern 3/4. Leipzig: Deutscher Verlag für Musik, 1975. P.177, facs. Nos.23, 26, trans. No.23.

Stainer, John. *Early Bodleian Music.* 3 vols. London, 1901; reprint Farnborough: Gregg, 1967. Vol. 1, Plate 7, facs. No.2.

Ulsamer, Josef, and Klaus Stahmer. *Musikalisches Tafelkonfekt.* Würzburg: Sturtz, 1973. P.10, facs. and trans. No.23.

Werf, Hendrik van der. "Estampie," *The New Grove Dictionary of Music and Musicians,* 20 vols. London: MacMillan, 1981. Vol. VI, p.255, facs. Nos.4–6, trans. Nos.1a, 4, 16.

Wolf, Johannes. *Handbuch der Notationskunde.* 2 vols. Leipzig: Breitkopf & Härtel, 1913. Vol. I, p.224, facs. Nos.39–41; pp.225–27, 234–35, trans. Nos.2, 39. Vol. II, p.9, facs. Nos.42–44; pp.9–11, trans. No.44.

––––––. "Die Tänze des Mittelalters," *Archiv für Musikwissenschaft* I (1918–19):10–42, trans. Nos.2, 14–28, 31–34, 39–41.

Wooldridge, Harry E. *Early English Harmony, from the 10th to the 15th Century.* London: Stainer and Bell, 1897. Vol. I, Plates 18, 19, 42, 43, facs. Nos.2, 39–44.